# Vedic Astrology

**Bibliothèque et Archives nationales du Québec and Library and Archives Canada cataloguing in publication**

Leclerc, Andrée, 1962-
Vedic astrology : fate and free will

(Approach)

ISBN 978-2-922417-65-4

1. Hindu astrology. 2. Birth charts. 3. Vedanta. I. Title.

BF1714.H5L4213 2011 133.5'9445 C2011-941619-0

Legal deposit
Bibliothèque nationale du Québec
National Library of Canada

Distributed in Canada by:
Distribution du livre Mirabel (ERPI-DLM)
5757 rue Cypihot
Saint-Laurent (Quebec) H4S 1R3
Canada
Tel: 514-334-2690 / 1-800-263-3678
Fax: 514 334-4720 / 1-800-643-4720
www.erpi.com

Distributed in the USA by:
Enfield Publishing & Distribution Co.
P.O. Box 699
Enfield, New Hampshire 03748
United States
Tel: 603-632-7377
Fax: 603-632-5611
www.enfieldbooks.com

Government of Québec — Tax credit for book publishing Administrated by SODEC

Translation assistance program: SODEC



Translation from French (Canada): Jan Brzezinski
Cover design and Page layout: Manon Léveillé

Printed in Canada


www.iqe.qc.ca

1 2 3 4 5 13 12 11

Andrée Leclerc

# Vedic Astrology

Fate and Free will

*Preface by Robert A. Koch*

IQ

*Approach*

# THE SERIES

Titles published in the *Approach* series aim at broadening our understanding of spirituality and making the rich content of the *Vedas*—the founding texts of the oldest philosophical tradition in the world—readily available to all. From the dawn of time, great masters have faithfully transmitted this science, each in their turn delivering the keys to knowing the self, the universe, and the Ultimate Reality. The original texts and the teachings derived from them are meant for humanity as a whole, without distinction as to race, culture, or beliefs. They provide invaluable answers to our most fundamental questions, and all who have approached them with an open mind have received the greatest benefits. That is why we have chosen to present them in a series that is both accessible to everyone, including younger readers, and representative of this vast compendium of universal knowledge and wisdom.

As the *Vedas* were originally written in Sanskrit, our authors occasionally refer to names or concepts that have no direct equivalent in English. Where appropriate, these Sanskrit words have been spelt just as they should be pronounced rather than with diacritical marks and letter combinations that are sometimes difficult to decipher. We hope that purists will not take offense, but will support our effort, which aims at accessibility rather than scholarship.

Those interested in the subject of the books in this series can directly submit their questions and comments by email to: *comments@approachseries.com.*

# TABLE OF CONTENTS

# PREFACE

## Vedic Astrology, Destiny, and Free Will

The philosophical principles of destiny and fate have been the constructs of thinking in most cultures since antiquity. However, the apparent opposing concept of free will has raised some controversies in the minds of modern thinkers, many of whom insist that one can do whatever he or she wants given the proper mental attitude or resolve. While fate and free will may seem to be conflicting principles, in fact, they are one and the same and one cannot exist without the other.

Vedic astrology, cosmology, and philosophy in general hold to the principle of karma, whereby one assumes accountability to the results of actions performed previously, whether in this or prior lifetimes. Free will is the central underpinning of the *atma*, or soul, who by his nature aspires to achieve something, whether it is within the framework of the temporary material world, or that of the eternal, spiritual world. The controversy over which has the greater influence—fate or free will—would never occur to start with had the eternal and imperishable soul not been entangled in the temporal world wherein actions will always bring about their resultant material reactions. Thus in actuality, the true dilemma of the soul is not whether or not his free will can circumvent his fate, but rather that his material existence is illogical in the first place. It is illogical because he is trying to fulfill the desire for permanent happiness in a temporal place.

Therefore, one should consider the difference between the true or eternal aspect of the self, and the false identity that he assumes within the framework of matter. The consideration of these differences, in the opinion of the Vedic *Upanishads* (corollary scriptures), is the beginning of self-realization. The path of self-realization as per Vedic philosophy causes one to ponder such dual concepts as "truth vs. falsehood", "reality vs. illusion", "permanence vs. non-permanence", etc. If one can reason that if everything within this world is temporary, and if attachment to temporary matter is the cause of repeated birth and deaths in material forms, then he can also reason that he is responsible for enjoying or suffering the results of his actions lifetime after lifetime. His assuming responsibility for the results of actions comes in the form of fate, or destiny, the timings for which are identifiable in the Vedic astrological chart.

So does destiny imply that one can do nothing about the conditions of life in which he finds himself? Certainly not, if the natural impulse of the soul is free will. In the same way that actions produce infinite and permanent possibilities in the spiritual world, so also in his true state of spiritual consciousness, the soul has unlimited free will in the matter of fulfilling desire. However, if the eternal soul insists on remaining within the temporal material realm, then free will is also limited and can be exercised only within the parameters that his karma or fate allows.

The analogy of the criminal may be helpful for understanding these principles. If someone commits a crime and is imprisoned, then his free will is curtailed. He still has free will, but he can fulfill it only within the restrictions of the prison cell within which he finds himself. Similarly, in some lifetime the embodied soul may commit a transgression over the rights and freedoms of others, thus setting up a prison sentence for himself in the next lifetime. If one kills another living being without the need for survival or self-defense, then he must be killed in a future lifetime. In all such lifetimes he has the free will to act or not, but what is certain is that in the future lifetime he will have to live within the four walls of his own karma.

With the current volume, Andrée Leclerc makes a courageous attempt not only to teach the basics of Vedic astrology, but to also underscore the above very important philosophical underpinnings of Vedic thought. Some persons may question whether the movements and prerogatives of the soul are that restricted in the modern world, or argue that the concept of destiny is part of an antiquated way of thinking. Others may say that the mind is the remote origin of one's actions and that if the mind is trained to contemplate ideal outcomes, then one can surmount the mandates of his karma and achieve such fulfillment. Such philosophies may be appealing, as one would always like to think that given a certain mental orientation, one could create whatever he likes. However, a careful study of the predictive systems in Vedic astrology will invariably produce convincing evidence that we are in fact recipients of the full range of good and bad reactions to prior actions, and that the timings for such are also written since the moment of birth.

Vedic astrology, however, does not leave one as a victim of his fate. There are a variety of remedial measures offered in the Vedic texts, such as spiritual rituals, mantras, charitable acts, wearing planetary gemstones, etc. which will help to alleviate the results of karma. Further, the knowledge of when and to what extent one will encounter the positive and negative experiences of life helps to give the mind pause as well as acceptance of the irrefutable interface between nature and its laws, and his own actions. A study of the Vedic horoscope will inadvertently produce a sense of humility and acceptance, and a reverence for the forces that be which put such natural laws in place. This kind of disposition is by far more conducive to enlightenment—the ultimate goal of human life—than the self-absorption or indignation that results from thinking that one can do whatever he likes in defiance of natural laws.

The Vedic astrological community welcomes this ground-breaking work of Andrée Leclerc, not only due to her thorough knowledge of practical Vedic astrology, but also due to her lifelong dedication to the Vedic way of life. The concepts of free will and destiny will thus emerge from these pages as not only philosophies, but organic realities that can be observed and replicated through Vedic astrology.

Robert A. Koch, Vedic Astrologer
Author, *The Spiritual Dimensions of Vedic Astrology*
www.robertkoch.com

# FOREWORD

## A Universal Culture

Vedic or Hindu astrology originates in India where it is called "the science of light" (*jyotish*) or "the science of time" (*kala-vidya*).

The word *veda* means "knowledge" in the ancient Sanskrit language, and we use the word Vedic to refer to everything connected to the world of the *Vedas*, a body of texts that contains millennia of accumulated wisdom. Thus if we specifically refer to "Vedic astrology," it is to emphasize the practical nature of the wisdom and insight that this particular science can provide.

## A Science Based in Wisdom

Traditionally, Vedic astrology was never used out of simple curiosity or for purely recreational purposes, as is often the case in the West. This system was created by the wise to help us acquire wisdom, by yogis who wished to help us progress in the practice of yoga, and by scholars to help us learn more about ourselves and the forces that affect us.

The *Vedas* encompass a very large universe. They not only deal with physical health and medicine, but also with internal development and the various types of yoga: the yoga of postures (*hatha yoga*), the yoga of action (*karma yoga*), the yoga of knowledge (*gyana yoga*) and the yoga of love and devotion (*bhakti yoga*).

Vedic astrology covers all these aspects of life and many others, and is often used in combination with other practices and approaches to wellness and fulfillment.

## Benefits of Vedic Astrology

Astrology is one of the important branches of Vedic knowledge. The beauty of Vedic astrology is that it gives us an immediate understanding of ourselves without our having to follow any yogic discipline, which often requires years of practice that would be particularly difficult for a Westerner. For example, the *Vedas* teach that without being a vegetarian and practicing meditation every day for an hour or two, no practice of yoga can be considered serious. Vedic astrology is therefore an exceptional way to access self-knowledge and the treasures of the Vedic culture.

With the help of a good Vedic astrologer we quickly get a clear vision of who we are, our position in this world, our potential and, most importantly, how we can make maximum use of our strengths, while at the same time helping us deal with the problems that are bound to arise in our lives. Vedic astrology can even gradually lead us to spiritual awakening and ultimate liberation.

## The Choice of Terms

Another reason we prefer the term "Vedic" astrology rather than "Indian" or "Hindu" is that India is a geographical territory, whereas Vedic astrology has never been limited to India alone.

The India we know today is only a small part of the Vedic world, which once extended to the West as far as Afghanistan and Pakistan, which split from India merely 60 years ago, and to the East as far as Bangladesh, Bhutan, Cambodia, Thailand, and even Indonesia. Moreover, vestiges of this culture, which have existed for thousands of years, can still be found in most of these regions.

The Vedic culture was even transmitted to the Far East, to China and Japan, through Buddhism, which also has its roots in the Vedic tradition. The founder of Buddhism in China, Bodhidharma, was often called "the old Hindu Yogi." Today, this culture is again spreading across the world. As a result, we can now find highly qualified yogis, Ayurvedic physicians and Vedic astrologers in the United States, Canada, Europe, and elsewhere.

In short, the term "Vedic" should be thought of as related to a mode of consciousness rather than a particular geographic location.

# INTRODUCTION

## Vedic Astrology – The Science of Light

We invite you to explore the great mysteries of life through the multidimensional prism of Vedic astrology. You will discover unsuspected inner worlds, unmask the dangers that lurk at life's shadowy crossroads, and learn to circumvent or overcome your karmic limitations. You will learn to know yourself more intimately and marvel at your heretofore hidden potential.

Since Vedic astrology is based in a profound wisdom, it offers you a new, impartial, and remarkably accurate way of looking at yourself, the consequences of your past, present, and future actions, the essence of your being, and the opportunities that await you.

For thousands of years, Vedic astrology has provided refreshing and instructive insights into people's lives by helping them identify factors related to:

- Their body and health;
- Character and personality;
- Intelligence type and natural tendencies;
- Skills, strengths, and weaknesses;
- Career choices;
- Prospects of success and enrichment;
- The emotional climate and relations with family, friends, and lovers;
- The influence of different time periods and planetary transits;

- The best times to carry out important activities;
- Finding answers to personal questions; and
- Possible antidotes to negative or stressful influences.

The astronomical coordinates at the time and place of a person's birth provide a map that is meant to help him navigate through life. The reading and interpretation of this map is both a science and an art, in that it requires the use of all the human mind's faculties of analysis and synthesis to get a clear vision and make appropriate judgments on the basis of data garnered from direct experience and repeatedly verified.

## Karma and Free Will

The whole philosophy of the *Vedas* is based on the concepts of the soul, reincarnation, and the law of karma, which means that our every action has a reaction. Our karma is manifested in every one of our traits, abilities or disabilities, particular interests, and the circumstances that we obtain in the course of our life. Because of karma, someone is born rich while another is poor; one person is beautiful and another ugly; or one is born in France, America, or India. And, our karma continues to follow us when we leave the body, for we carry it with us wherever we go. This means that for our karma to be fulfilled, we must take birth again.

We experience a portion of our karma each and every day, even while the greater part of it remains unconscious or latent, awaiting the right moment to become manifest in the way that a shadowy figure is revealed with the proper lighting. At the same time, while experiencing the results of some of our past and present deeds, we continue, through our every action, to accumulate other reactions that will mature and materialize in a future life.

Nevertheless, despite being caught in this network of actions and reactions governed by the laws of nature, we must also remain aware of our free will. We are in fact always free to choose our attachments, actions and attitudes, and this gives us some latitude to change—in part—our future karma.

Vedic astrology is specifically designed to give us a multidimensional view of life in this world by helping us understand our past, make the most of the present, and bring our immediate hopes and goals into harmony both with our nature and our deepest aspirations.

Everything in the universe is connected and nothing is left to chance, so that events, both happy and tragic, happen for a specific reason and purpose. Vedic astrology helps us to understand these phenomena and, in so doing, guides us on the path by which we will achieve our desired goals through maximizing our potential at any given time.

Since no phenomenon in the universe is isolated—whether the relations of cause and effect are apparent to us or not—it follows that every action has its reaction, since actions consist of energies that vibrate and reverberate all about. We are born, we grow up, and we act, and the very least of our actions has some influence around us. This is what we call the law of karma. This concept is also summarized in the Bible, "We reap what we sow." We should therefore seek to act in ways that best serve our real interests and those of our fellow humans, knowing that we will suffer for as long as we are not free of karma.

Moreover, through its analysis of the planetary periods and transits that affect our birth or natal chart, Vedic astrology can inform us about the type of karma that will dominate in every phase of our life. We can thus get ready, anticipating the moments of happiness and success that await us, or preparing ourselves for more difficult periods that may come at other times of our existence. Moreover, Vedic astrology also offers remedies or "antidotes" to our current and future challenging episodes, which we will discuss in the last chapter of this book.

## The *Vedas* and Astrology

Astrology is not an independent discipline, but rather a small part of a cultural, philosophical, and spiritual tradition that dates back to immemorial times. Compiled more than 3000 years before the Common Era, the *Vedas* are not the result of empirical research or intellectual knowledge. They were transmitted to us by wise intermediaries, or masters, in the form of "revealed" texts that originate with the Ultimate Source of all, the Absolute and Eternal Truth.

As one segment of this monument of wisdom, Vedic astrology aims to show us the way that will not only lead to release from karma, but also bring us knowledge and understanding of our higher nature. It portrays life in both its material and spiritual dimensions, and makes us capable of recognizing trends and predicting their development, while leaving us the ability to exercise our free will.

Without necessarily specifying the exact day or hour, a long-term forecast might take the following form: "Sometime after November 22 next year, your career will take off. This period will be conducive to your getting a promotion or a new job that will give you much more satisfaction than your current position. Your chances of success are also very high." More advanced calculations will also target important events in a much more specific way, if one seeks a higher degree of accuracy.

In the spirit of the *Vedas,* astrology ultimately serves to elevate the human being from the physical world—where the soul identifies with matter—to the spiritual world. In other words, it helps us getting free from all enslaving desires and discarding the attachments produced by ego, which cause us so much suffering, to make room for our true identity. All the techniques involved are designed to gradually disentangle us from our sufferings and to improve our situation in a sustainable manner.

## Basic Principles of Astronomy

As astrology is based on astronomy, an understanding of some basic principles of celestial mechanics is very useful. In this perspective, we will use the Earth as our point of observation.

The Earth's rotation over a 24-hour period gives us the impression of a uniform motion from east to west.

The backdrop of the sky is filled with so-called fixed stars that form constellations. In its apparent path around the Earth—since it is in fact the Earth that orbits the Sun—the Sun crosses the sky in a belt-like trajectory called the ecliptic. In doing so, it passes through 27 constellations, which are connected to the 12 signs of the zodiac.

Five celestial bodies visible to the naked eye also move on the ecliptic in their orbit around the Sun: Mercury, Venus, Mars, Jupiter, and Saturn. To these five planets we add the luminary bodies, the Sun and the Moon, and the two lunar nodes, Rahu and Ketu, which represent the northern and southern points of intersection of the Moon's path with the ecliptic. These nine entities or "planets"[1] are the active elements of the astrological chart. Uranus, Neptune, and Pluto are not considered essential in traditional Vedic astrology, even though references to these planets have been found in the texts of *Vasishta Nadi.*

The Sun moves along the ecliptic at a rate of about one degree every day, so that in one year, or exactly 365.2563 days, it crosses the full 360 degrees of arc corresponding to a sidereal year, or a complete revolution through the sphere of fixed stars. The planets, meanwhile, travel along the ecliptic on a circular band of 17 degrees, with the exception of Pluto, whose orbit is eccentric.

The Earth rotates on its axis, which is tilted at about 23°27′. It is this tilt that causes the phenomenon of seasons in the northern and southern hemispheres. The rotation of the Earth itself creates our days and

---

1. We use the term for the sake of simplification, since technically speaking, the Sun, the Moon, Rahu, and Ketu are not planets.

nights, while its rotation around the Sun gives us the impression, from our vantage point, that it is moving through the different constellations.

The twelve constellations of the zodiac found on the ecliptic are: Aries, Taurus, Gemini, Cancer, Leo, Virgo, Libra, Scorpio, Sagittarius, Capricorn, Aquarius, and Pisces. These constellations comprise what we call the zodiac, through which the planets move.

The equator is the geometric line that divides the Earth into two equal hemispheres. If we extend it into infinity, we get an imaginary line that is called the "celestial equator." And its line of intersection with the ecliptic becomes what is called the line of the equinoxes.

The tropical zodiac generally used in Western astrology is defined from the vernal point, which is the point of the ecliptic where the Sun is situated on the day of the spring equinox. Vedic astrology, by contrast, is based on the sidereal zodiac, or the zodiac of fixed stars. Because of the astronomical phenomenon known as the "precession of the equinoxes," the vernal point glides slowly along the ecliptic under the gravity that the Sun, the Moon, and the planets exercise over the Earth, which vacillates like a top around the pole of the ecliptic.

Due to this gliding effect, the first day of spring no longer corresponds to the beginning of the sign of Aries as it is observed on the canvas of fixed stars. This phenomenon gradually produces a gap that amounts to 1 degree every 72 years and thus of 30 degrees—which corresponds to a complete zodiac sign—in 2160 years.

Presently, the difference between the tropical and the sidereal zodiac is 24 degrees for the year 2011. Over the thousands of years that are to follow, the vernal point will successively be under the influence of the 12 signs of the sidereal zodiac, taking some 26,000 years to cross all the signs before returning to 0 degree of Aries, where it will correspond once again to the spring equinox.

## I Have to Change Signs?

Because of this astronomical singularity, in Vedic astrology, the majority of people see their Ascendant and some of their planets move back one sign from the conventional western system. Needless to say, this makes a considerable difference! The precision that results is more than just symbolic: it makes it possible to interpret factual cosmic influences revealed by the celestial chart.

We now have many computer programs designed to perform the calculations necessary for astrologers to establish a birth chart. The only data required are the following: the date and time of birth, and the geographic coordinates of one's birthplace. We need not, therefore, go into the details of these calculations. Instead, we will point you to free yet very complete and easy to use online or downloadable programs so that you can obtain your Vedic chart and directly follow and apply the explanations in this book. To access them, please go to *www.yourvedicastrology.com/book1.*

## Two Ways of Mapping Birth Charts

Two kinds of diagrams are used to represent the Vedic astrological chart, one from South India and the other from North India.

Here below you can see a South Indian chart. In this representation, the signs of the zodiac are fixed and therefore always occupy the same location. The planets are arranged according to their position in the celestial sphere at a given time, and the houses (indicated by numbers) follow each other in a clockwise direction from the Ascendant. The chart shown is that of Jim Morrison.

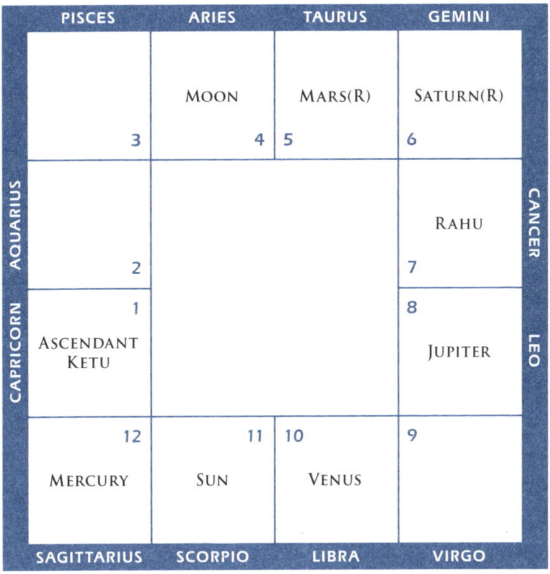


South Indian layout

The next diagram is of the same chart presented in the North Indian format. In this case, it is the houses that are fixed. Thus the angles (also called "quadrants" or "*kendras*"), which are the houses of power—1, 4, 7, and 10—are located respectively in the North, West, South, and East of the diagram. The Ascendant always holds the square to the North (i.e., at the top of the chart), and the signs, like the houses, follow one another in counterclockwise direction. Again, the numbers 1 through 12 refer to the houses.

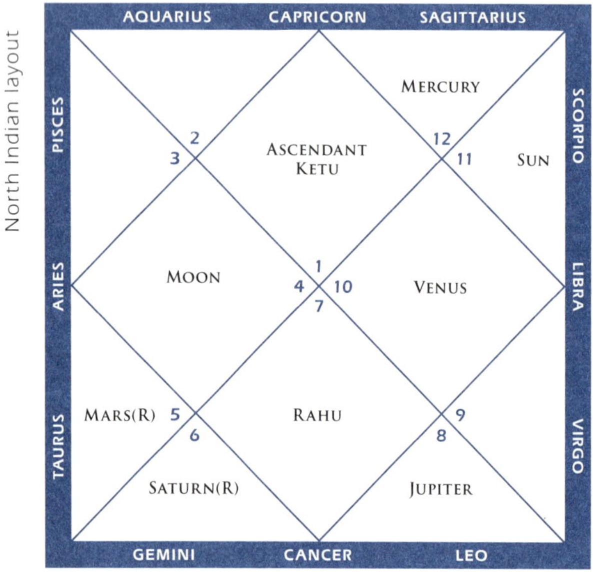


Throughout this work, we have chosen to present both representations of each chart next to each other so you can use the one with which you feel most comfortable. The planets and signs will be identified by name, but where possible, we will also familiarize you with their symbols as we go through the text.

A birth chart can also be accompanied by a Moon chart—in which the sign occupied by the Moon takes the place of the Ascendant. Another kind of chart is based on the 9th division of the birth chart, which is used to verify and to confirm the various indications of the horoscope. We shall come back to this later.

# CHAPTER 1

# THE PLANETS

So, let's start by looking at the active elements of the chart!

The sage Parashara says:

> The Creator of the universe has many *avatars*, which include the nine planets in which forms He manifests Himself in order to grant all living beings the results of their karma. In these forms, He destroys the negative energies and supports the positive ones.
>
> *Brihat Parashara Hora Shastra*

So we should not think of the planets as mere lumps of inert matter. They are vested with powers to rule over all aspects of what we call "astrology", and to determine the characteristics of the signs and houses they govern.

## EACH PLANET HAS ITS OWN PERSONALITY

Each planet thus has its own personality, with its own preferences, indifferences, and strengths through association with other planets, signs, or houses, as well as its age of maturation—that is, the time when it becomes capable of fully manifesting its influence, its hierarchical position among its peers, and so on.

The following tables summarize the characteristics of each of the planets.

| Planet/ Symbol | Related Sign(s) | Friendly Planets | Inimical Planet(s) | Neutral Planet(s) |
|---|---|---|---|---|
| Sun ☉ | Leo | Jupiter<br>Mars<br>Moon | Venus<br>Saturn | Mercury |
| Moon ☽ | Cancer | Sun<br>Mercury | None | Mars<br>Venus<br>Saturn<br>Jupiter |
| Mercury ☿ | Gemini<br>Virgo | Sun<br>Venus | Moon | Mars<br>Jupiter<br>Saturn |
| Venus ♀ | Taurus<br>Libra | Mercury<br>Saturn | Moon<br>Sun | Mars<br>Jupiter |
| Mars ♂ | Aries<br>Scorpio | Sun<br>Moon<br>Jupiter | Mercury | Venus<br>Saturn |
| Jupiter ♃ | Sagittarius<br>Pisces | Sun<br>Moon<br>Mars | Mercury<br>Venus | Saturn |
| Saturn ♄ | Capricorn<br>Aquarius | Mercury<br>Venus | Sun<br>Moon<br>Mars | Jupiter |
| Rahu ☊ | Aquarius (if stronger than Saturn) | Jupiter<br>Venus<br>Saturn | Sun<br>Moon<br>Mars | Mercury |
| Ketu ☋ | Scorpio (if stronger than Mars) | Mars<br>Venus<br>Saturn | Sun<br>Moon | Mercury<br>Jupiter |

Like us, the planets feel more at ease to express their nature and characteristics when they are positively associated with their friends. From a relational point of view, there are two major groups of planets: the higher entities, namely the Sun, Moon, Mars, and Jupiter, and the lower entities, comprising Saturn, Venus, and Mercury. We will see that these two groups are connected by the arrangement of the houses from the Ascendant.

## The Planets' Ups and Downs

The strength of each planet depends on several factors. Among these, its location in the zodiac is one of the most important, because when it is exalted, for example, it displays its attributes more easily, for better or for worse. Conversely, when it is debilitated, we are forced to make further efforts to achieve results or avoid problems.

### Debilitation

The debilitation sign or "sign of fall" for each planet is the one that most opposes its intrinsic nature. Nonetheless, this does not necessarily mean that it becomes completely negative, because aspects from benefic planets may also help such a planet better express itself.

Let us elaborate a bit on each of the planets in this context.

- **Sun**: As the Sun represents the ego, when it is in the sociable sign of Libra, it must make more room for others, something that it does not find altogether natural.

- **Moon**: The Moon stands for emotions and perceptions. In the secret and passionate sign of Scorpio, these can become turbulent and indicate a person ruled by instinct. On the other hand, it might also open the door to extrasensory perceptions.

- **Mercury**: As a worthy representative of rational thinking, Mercury is not at all comfortable in Pisces, the realm of intuition.

- **Venus**: Ah, love! It would be harder to see Venus flourish in Virgo, where everything is analyzed and calculated to meticulous perfection.

- **Mars**: The planet of action and initiative par excellence may feel awkward in Cancer, which is all tenderness, kindness, and consideration for others, and where one may even take refuge in a make-believe world, if need be.

- **Jupiter**: The blessed and compassionate Jupiter is exalted in Cancer, but not in Capricorn, where hard work and the pursuit of power are the order of the day.

- **Saturn**: Saturn the taciturn, firm in practice and perseverance, feels that the passion and courage of Aries do not go well with its nature.

| Planet/ Symbol | Exaltation Sign/Point | Comfort Zone | Power Zone | Debilitation Sign/Point |
|---|---|---|---|---|
| Sun ☉ | Aries (10°) | Leo | Leo (0-20°) | Libra (10°) |
| Moon ☽ | Taurus (3°) | Cancer | Taurus (4-30°) | Scorpio (3°) |
| Mercury ☿ | Virgo (15°) | Gemini Virgo | Virgo (15-20°) | Pisces (15°) |
| Venus ♀ | Pisces (27°) | Taurus Libra | Libra (0-15°) | Virgo (27°) |
| Mars ♂ | Capricorn (28°) | Aries Scorpio | Aries (0-12°) | Cancer (28°) |
| Jupiter ♃ | Cancer (5°) | Sagittarius Pisces | Sagittarius (0-10°) | Capricorn (5°) |
| Saturn ♄ | Libra (20°) | Capricorn Aquarius | Aquarius (0-20°) | Aries (20°) |
| Rahu ☊ | Taurus | Taurus Gemini | None | Scorpio Sagittarius |
| Ketu ☋ | Scorpio | Scorpio Sagittarius | None | Taurus Gemini |

- **Rahu**: Rahu is so full of desire and the quest for scientific evidence confirming the benefits of materialism that it does not know how to appreciate the highly idealistic Sagittarius or the secretly passionate and dedicated Scorpio.

- **Ketu**: Ketu wants to be released from material desires and pleasures, and so is uncomfortable in the materialistic sign of Taurus, which is focused on acquisition, or in that of Gemini, which is intent on business, social life, and communication.

## The Significator of the Soul

In the last table we saw that the planets are sensitive to the exact position they occupy degree-wise. Let us look a little more closely at this issue to determine what planet in a person's chart best represents him and characterizes his approach to life in the present incarnation. This planet happens to be the one positioned at the highest degree, regardless of which sign it is in. When looking at the soul significator, we must pay particular attention to the influences it receives from other planets.

In this connection, it should be noted that Rahu and Ketu are always retrograde, i.e., they move backwards, which means that if they are at 29° of a sign, they have only just entered it, whereas at 1°, they are about to leave. As each sign contains 30 degrees, we should apply the following reasoning: if Venus is at 28°49′ and Rahu at 1°, then Rahu will be the soul significator, because 30 – 1 = 29, which is greater than

| Planet/ Symbol | House of Power | House of Fall | Age of Maturation | Social Group and Status |
|---|---|---|---|---|
| Sun ☉ | 10 | 12 | 22 years | **King**<br>Warrior |
| Moon ☽ | 4 | 8 | 24 years | **Queen**<br>Merchant<br>Farmer |
| Mercury ☿ | 1 | 4 | 32 years | **Prince**<br>Merchant<br>Farmer |
| Venus ♀ | 4 | 6 | 25 years | **Advisor**<br>Priest<br>Scholar |
| Mars ♂ | 10 | 7 | 28 years | **Commander**<br>Warrior |
| Jupiter ♃ | 1 | 3 | 16 years | **Advisor**<br>Priest<br>Scholar |
| Saturn ♄ | 7 | 1 | 36 years | **Servant**<br>Worker |
| Rahu ☊ | N.A. | 9 | 42 years | No defined social role |
| Ketu ☋ | N.A. | 3 | 48 years | No defined social role |

28°49′. Note, moreover, that Ketu never acts as the soul significator.

Each planet's attributes flourish when it is in its house of power and diminish in its house of fall. Note that these rules apply only to the position of the planets starting from the natural Ascendant as opposed to the Ascendant of the Moon chart or the 9th division chart. We will return to this later.

Each planet reaches maturation at the age when its influence becomes fully manifest in one's life, for better or for worse. This phenomenon is particularly noticeable when a planet occupies a prominent position in the chart. Moreover, as each planet takes some time to reach maturation, it occurs at different times in one's life. For example, a person with Jupiter well placed in his chart will have a naturally flourishing optimism in his 16th year. However, since this optimism is combined with a lack of life experience, his parents may have to deal with a teenager who is a bit too optimistic and idealistic, if not unrealistic.

## Social Group and Status

This characteristic mainly shows how each planet works or "thinks." We can expect to see it become prominent when a planet is strong and well placed in a chart, and less prominent when the planet is very afflicted.

For example, the priest or scholar, i.e., the intellectual type, is normally attracted to teaching or ritual activities, whereas the warrior type will more likely act as a law officer or as a defender of society. Similarly, merchants and farmers will probably have something to promote or sell, while the servant, craftsman, or artist will labour in the service of the other groups.

The lunar nodes are excluded, for their part, from any such classification of occupational duty, or indeed any definitive orientation. They can therefore cause various disturbances in society and even threaten the established order.

## Relations Between Planets

### Aspects

In addition to occupying a specific zodiac sign and a house, the planets also "look" at other signs and houses. This form of looking is called an "aspect" in astrology. By its aspects, each planet exerts its influence, sometimes on a planet, sometimes on a sign or a house, the effects of which will be triggered at the appropriate time.

To identify the aspects of a planet, we must start from the space in which it is located and count from there. In the following list, the house or houses that each planet aspects are listed:

- ☉ Sun: 7th house
- ☽ Moon: 7th house
- ☿ Mercury: 7th house
- ♀ Venus: 7th house
- ♂ Mars: 4th, 7th, and 8th houses
- ♃ Jupiter: 5th, 7th, and 9th houses
- ♄ Saturn: 3th, 7th, and 10th houses

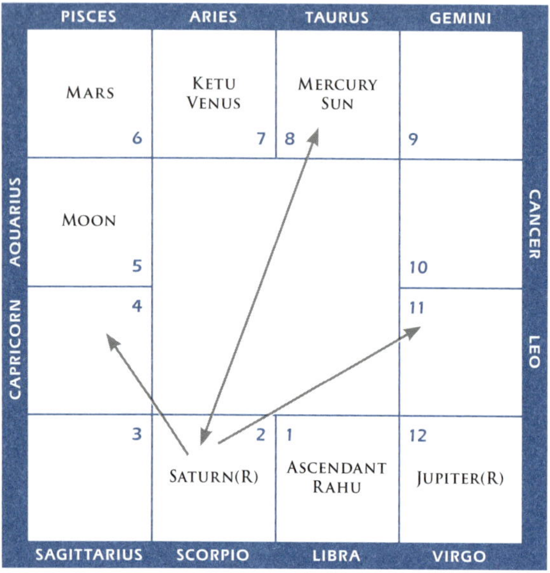
PISCES
ARIES
TAURUS
GEMINI
MARS
6
KETU
VENUS
7
MERCURY
SUN
8
9
AQUARIUS
MOON
5
CANCER
10
CAPRICORN
4
LEO
11
3
2
SATURN(R)
1
ASCENDANT
RAHU
12
JUPITER(R)
SAGITTARIUS
SCORPIO
LIBRA
VIRGO

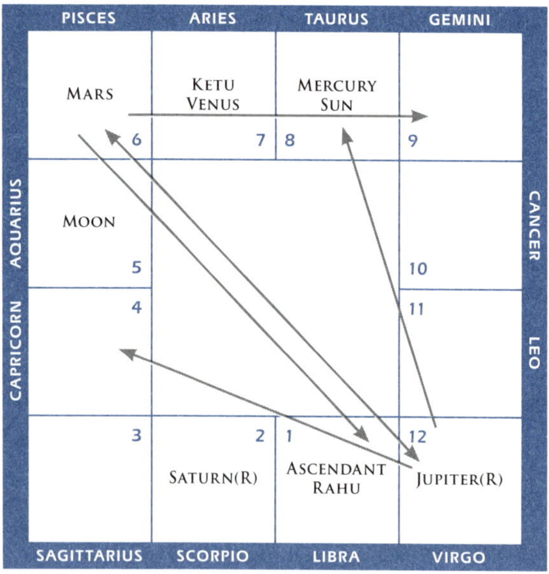
PISCES
ARIES
TAURUS
GEMINI
MARS
6
KETU
VENUS
7
MERCURY
SUN
8
9
AQUARIUS
MOON
5
CANCER
10
CAPRICORN
4
LEO
11
3
2
SATURN(R)
1
ASCENDANT
RAHU
12
JUPITER(R)
SAGITTARIUS
SCORPIO
LIBRA
VIRGO

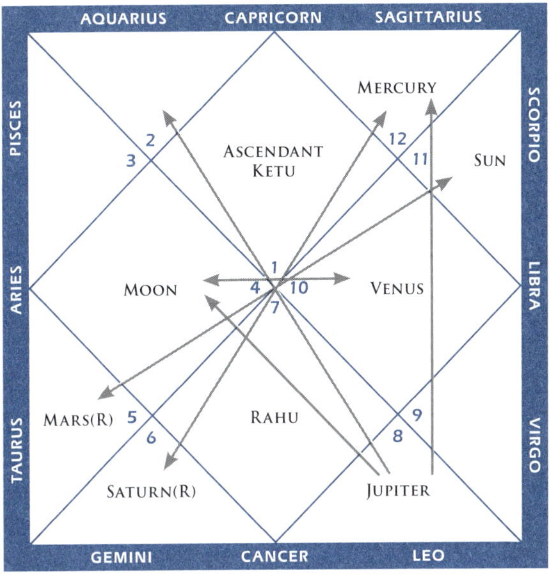


Aspects of the planets – The North Indian chart

☊ Rahu: 5th, 7th, and 9th houses

☋ Ketu: 5th, 7th, and 9th houses

THE SOUTH INDIAN CHARTS

In the examples given here, the Sun aspects Saturn and vice versa. Saturn also aspects the 3rd and 10th houses from its position (that is, houses 4 and 11).

Jupiter and Mars aspect one another. In addition, Mars aspects the 4th and 8th houses from its position, and Jupiter, the 5th and 9th houses.

THE NORTH INDIAN CHART

The Moon and Venus aspect each other, as do Mars and the Sun, as well as Mercury and Saturn. From the 8th house, Jupiter aspects houses 12, 2, and 4.

## Benefic or Malefic?

Each planet has either a benefic or malefic nature. Its intrinsic nature can be enhanced, modified, or overruled by other factors, but it is important to consider initially.

### Natural Benefics

The naturally benefic planets are Jupiter, Venus, Mercury (when properly associated), and the Moon in its waxing phase, or at least 90 degrees from the Sun when in its waning phase. The favourable location of the naturally benefic planets generally produces desirable outcomes, and their aspects contribute to the development of the attributes of the planets, houses, and signs that benefit from them.

### Natural Malefics

The naturally malefic planets are Saturn, Mars, the Sun, Rahu, Ketu, Mercury (when associated with other malefics and deprived of benefic influences), and the waning Moon when located less than 90 degrees—i.e., three houses or less—from the Sun. The new Moon phase is held to be particularly malefic.

When favourably located, malefics can also produce desirable results, but only after much effort, time, or struggle. Their aspects may also impede the functions of affected planets, houses, and signs.

When planets come together in the same sign, they are said to be in conjunction. They influence each other in addition to acting on the attributes of the sign and the house in which they are located.

When two planets are face to face, that is to say 7 signs or houses away from each other, they are said to be in opposition. They then mutually aspect one another.

The special aspects of Mars, Saturn, Jupiter, Rahu, and Ketu have as much influence as in the case of opposition, although in this scenario, the favour of an aspect is not necessarily returned.

It should be mentioned here that the natural malefics tend to exert their influence aggressively, while the benefic planets do not like confrontation. Thus, when natural malefics produce conjunctions or aspects, it is very likely that it will result in irritations, even if they rule good houses in the horoscope. The benefic planets, however, tend to make things easier.

## Particular Conditions

### Retrogradation (R)

A planet becomes retrograde when its movement across the sky appears to be backwards. Only Mercury, Venus, Mars, Jupiter, and Saturn can be retrograde. The Sun and the Moon always move forward, whereas Rahu and Ketu are always retrograde inasmuch as they move in the opposite direction of the other planets.

Several effects are attributed to retrogradation. Here are the most documented:

- A retrograde planet becomes more unpredictable, as if it were in conjunction with Rahu.

- A retrograde planet may be stronger or weaker than a normal planet.

- Retrograde planets produce delayed effects.

When a planet is in the process of turning retrograde or going back to its normal motion, there are a few days where it stops moving either way and appears as a stationary element amidst the normal movement of celestial activity. Such a planet thus becomes a focal point in the sky, which is said to amplify its natural dispositions. A planet in this state is referred to as "stationed."

## Combustion (C)

Combustion occurs when one or more planets are found in the neighbourhood of the Sun. When a planet is within 10 degrees of the Sun, the combustion is more pronounced. This condition weakens the affected planets—which are then said to be "combust"—and the houses they govern.

Note that Mercury is never very far from the Sun, and that combustion affects it less than it would other planets, such as Jupiter or Saturn.

A combust planet will continue to show its attributes on an intellectual or interior level, but its ability to express itself externally will be reduced. For example, a person with a combust Mercury will not see his intelligence fade—quite the contrary—but will probably be less sociable and talkative than if Mercury were not combust.

The planets affect our consciousness, each with its own particular colouring. We here give you the characteristics of each of them in their pure state, followed by examples to help you synthesize everything.

## THE SUN (*SURYA*) – "I AM"

King and master in our corner of the universe, the Sun keeps all the other planets in their orbit, and its intense fire has the power to purify our minds. By far the largest of the planets, it governs all that is great—trees, mountains, rocks—as well as all manifestations of power—monarchs, governments, centralized management, etc.

People of the Sun type have generally good health, good digestion and circulation, as well as the ability to burn toxins and pathogens through their fire energy. They have bright eyes and a radiant, golden, or somewhat rosy complexion, and are of medium height, strong, and muscular. Given their natural heat, they function better in cool climates.

Solar types command respect and are generally noble, strong, and capable of leadership. Proud, critical, and somewhat fixed in their opinions, they love being the center of attention and radiating on everyone around them.

In the charts of such people, the Sun occupies a dominant position in the Ascendant or one of the three other quadrants (houses 1, 4, 7, and 10), and becomes even stronger if it is in Leo or exalted in Aries and accompanied by naturally benefic planets.

## The Sun's Attributes

REPRESENTATIONS

Father, king, government, leaders, employers, health professionals, entrepreneurs, the ego.

SIGNIFICATIONS

Authority, nobility, creativity, generosity, power, masculinity, individuality.

POSITIVE ATTRIBUTES

Ambition, self-confidence, dignity, strength, willpower, courage, stability, ability to lead.

NEGATIVE ATTRIBUTES

Despotism, arrogance, selfishness, pride, ostentation, love of luxury, vanity, lack of subtlety, irritability, lack of vitality and magnetism, carelessness, lack of ideals.

FIELDS OF ACTION

Acquisition of knowledge, career, rational thought.

OUTCOMES SOUGHT

Glory and honour.

PHYSIOLOGY

The Sun rules the head, heart, skeleton, sight (especially in the right eye), vitality, and the red blood cells that carry oxygen and nourishment throughout the body. The Sun type is of average size.

PREFERRED PLACES

Forests, mountains, the East, castles, temples, and churches.

PREFERRED TIMES

Sunday.

METHOD OF PERSUASION

The rod.

GEMS, SEMI-PRECIOUS STONES, AND METALS

Ruby, spinel, garnet, sunstone, red zircon, red tourmaline, and copper.

### Sun-Type Celebrities

Paramahansa Yogananda, Elton John, Bill Clinton, Al Pacino, Mother Teresa, Robert Redford, Napoleon I, Madonna.

THE BIRTH CHART OF MADONNA

The Ascendant is in Leo with the Moon and Mercury. The Sun occupies the 12th house, which is ruled by the Moon. This may seem contradictory, except that the Sun and the Moon are occupying each other's houses, creating a yoga that unites them both.

The ex-queen of pop music cannot stop herself from thinking big and making every effort to achieve her ambitions. Nobody would deny that she has lots of energy and bright eyes, or that she is proud and dramatic, and likes to draw attention to herself. She is also both courageous and concerned with the plight of suffering humanity.

## The Moon (*Chandra*) – "Unconditional love"

The surface of the Moon, which intensely reflects the Sun's light, is also dotted with craters that are the

Natal chart — Madonna

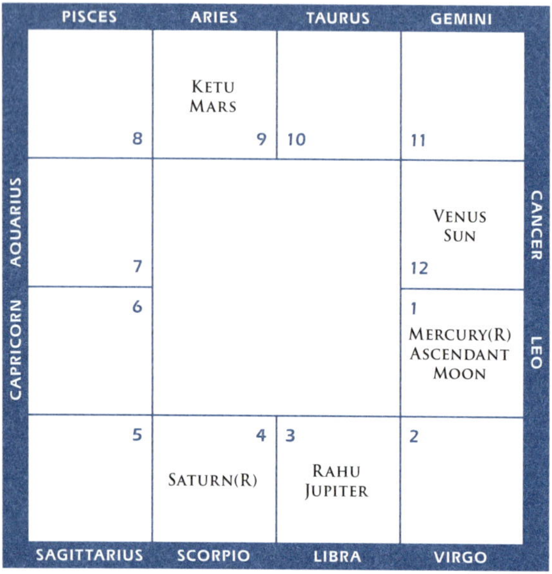


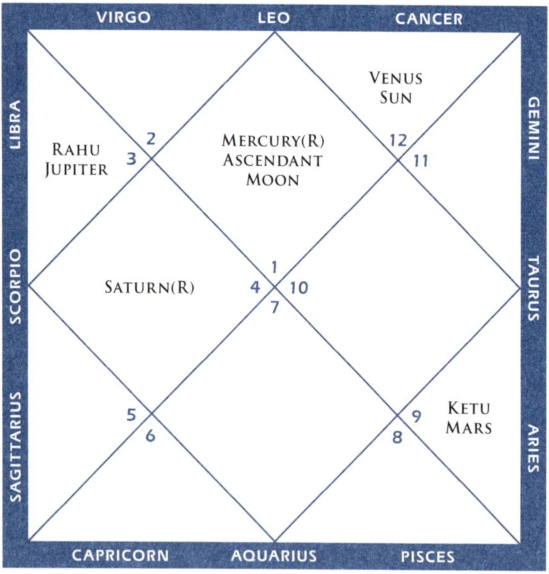

remnants of its past. In fact, the Moon represents the mind, which experiences and remembers easily, especially when the memories are painful. It orbits the Earth and always faces it.

The Moon also represents all that sparkles and glitters, cleanliness, the feelings expressed in a gaze, the experience of everything. As the source of reflected and indirect energy, it also indicates the people watching us—the public. The Moon manifests as the queen, as well as those who need more care, like seniors or babies.

The dominant element of Moon-types is water, which gives them a round and attractive face, a pale and clear complexion, and eyes with pronounced whites. Since these people have plenty of fluids, their bodies are well developed and their hair is often thick, shiny, and oily. This abundance of fluid also means that with age there is a tendency to gain weight and retain water. Laziness and too much sleep can also affect the Lunar types' health.

Naturally maternal, sociable, and loving, they like to take care of other people and help them. Keenly interested in human interactions, their loyal, friendly, and romantic disposition tend to make them good marriage partners, although they could also turn out being passive, shy, emotional, and sentimental.

On another level, people of the Moon type can be talented leaders, administrators, or diplomats, and possess great intuition, the gift of healing, and other psychic powers.

Of great importance in the birth chart, the Moon indicates the quality of the mind and the stability of emotions and perceptions. The Moon's positive qualities suffer when it receives influences from both Saturn and Mars simultaneously, or is placed alongside Rahu, which indicates mental turbulence or psychological problems such as phobias and obsessions.

The Lunar type is often found when the Moon occupies the Ascendant or one of the other quadrants (houses 1, 4, 7, and 10), particularly when in its own sign, Cancer, or in its sign of exaltation, Taurus. The Cancer Ascendant can also produce a Lunar type if the Moon is not dominated by other planets. If in conjunction with or aspected by Jupiter, the Lunar characteristics are reinforced. The Moon is particularly benefic when it is full or waxing and at a distance of at least 90 degrees from the Sun. When it is too close to the Sun, however, the Moon actually becomes malefic.

## The Moon's Attributes

### REPRESENTATIONS
Mother, queen, woman, the cook, the public.

### SIGNIFICATIONS
Happiness, common sense, emotions, early childhood, feelings, intellect, mind, memory.

### POSITIVE ATTRIBUTES
Good habits, responsiveness, sensitivity, imagination, fertility, gentleness, patience, morality, courtesy, sincerity, love of poetry, history, and travel.

### NEGATIVE ATTRIBUTES
Hypersensitivity, anxiety, instability, overreaction, evasiveness, difficulty of expression, shyness, unconsciousness.

FIELDS OF ACTION

Nourishing and protecting.

OUTCOMES SOUGHT

Growth and prosperity.

PHYSIOLOGY

The Moon governs the body fluids, chest, face, stomach, mental illness, sight (especially in the left eye), and everything that is cyclical. The Lunar type tends to have a small physique.

PREFERRED PLACES

At home, the North, near rivers or bodies of water, close to animals.

PREFERRED TIMES

Night, Monday.

METHOD OF PERSUASION

Temptation.

GEMS, SEMI-PRECIOUS STONES, AND METALS

Pearl, moonstone, silver.

## Moon-Type Celebrities

Buddha, Mahatma Gandhi, Barbara Streisand, Charlton Heston, Clint Eastwood, Brigitte Bardot, Yves Rocher.

THE BIRTH CHART OF CLINT EASTWOOD

The Moon occupies its own sign in the 10th house, while the Sun is in Taurus, the Moon's exaltation sign, and in the constellation of Rohini, a star ruled by the Moon.

Throughout his career, as actor, director, or politician, Clint Eastwood has lived in the public eye,

Natal chart — Clint Eastwood

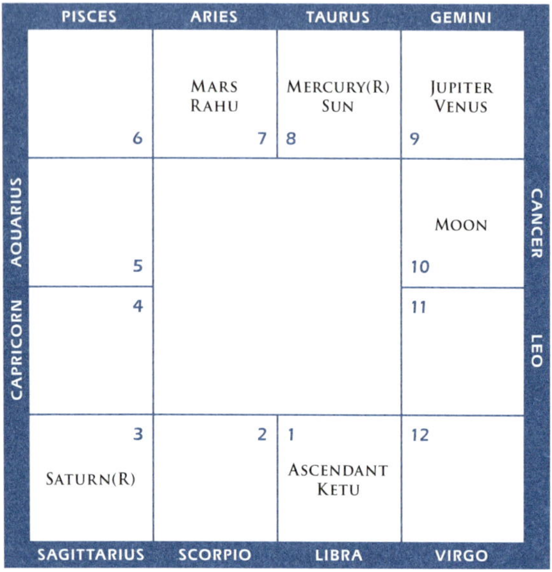


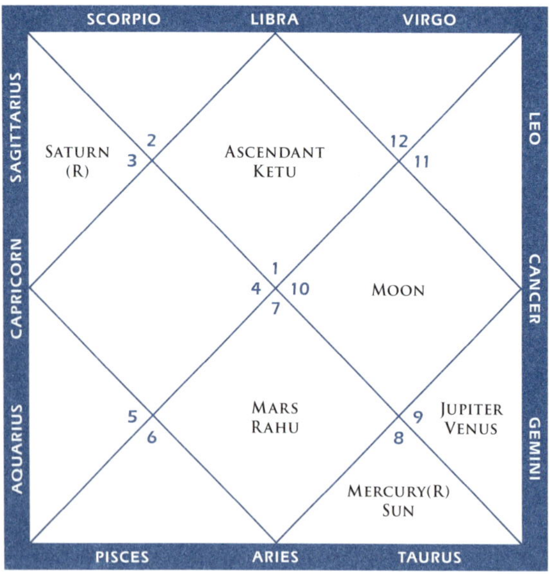

and we can safely attribute to him a sure instinct, a good imagination, and dependable administrative and organizational skills.

### MERCURY (*BUDHA*) – "THE LOGIC OF THINGS"

The tiny planet Mercury has the fastest orbit around the Sun. One side always faces the Sun and is very hot, the other is very cold; this makes people of the Mercury type comfortable in extreme conditions and quite adaptable—sometimes too much so when in bad company. Its speed, which gives it the mental agility needed to quickly sense impressions, changes when it turns retrograde, which gives it the opportunity to revisit the terrain it has already covered. Mercury is in fact considered more powerful when retrograde.

As the prince in the hierarchy of planets, Mercury is in the entourage of the Sun, having easy access to it, like a prince to the king. Since it is the most discriminating of the planets, Mercurians are usually intellectual and communicative. Whether tall or short, they tend to be thin and retain a youthful appearance. And, despite the sensitivity of their nervous and digestive systems, they can become good athletes, though they have less endurance than a Martian, especially as their heart and lungs are often fragile.

Mercurian types are intelligent, good communicators and talkers; they love to juggle with information and ideas. They know how to show empathy and humour, and can be very witty, though their intense mental activity can sometimes make them introverted.

Among their many interests are business and commerce, rigorous bookkeeping, a constant search for harmony and a desire to contribute to the welfare of others. Finally, it should be noted that they often have difficulty making decisions and then following through on them.

In the charts of people of this type, Mercury is dominant in the Ascendant or one of the three other quadrants, especially in Virgo or Gemini, and preferably influenced by other naturally benefic planets.

### Mercury's Attributes

#### REPRESENTATIONS

The world of human beings, living creatures, maternal uncles and aunts, scholars, secretaries, merchants, Vishnu.

#### SIGNIFICATIONS

Consciousness, faculties of analysis and diagnosis, discrimination, paper and books, poetry, language, and knowledge.

#### POSITIVE ATTRIBUTES

Confidence, humour, rationality, sharp intelligence, subtlety, ingenuity, skilfulness—particularly verbal and mental skills—excellent memory, eternal youth, versatility.

#### NEGATIVE ATTRIBUTES

A calculating attitude, detachment, difficulty in thinking and communicating clearly, unfeeling intellectuality, volatile or unstable character, selfishness, fickleness, deceit, falsehood, eccentricity, depravity, critical tendency, lack of education, culture, courtesy, and diplomacy.

#### FIELDS OF ACTION

Astrology, business, trade, communications, drawing, education, publishing, chemistry, pharmaceutics, medicine, mathematics, writing, design, counselling.

OUTCOMES SOUGHT

Understanding through a pragmatic approach.

PHYSIOLOGY

Mercury rules the intestines, intellect, speech, lungs, the nervous system and its disorders. The Mercurian type can be tall or short.

PREFERRED PLACES

The Earth, the East.

PREFERRED TIMES

Wednesday, short trips.

METHOD OF PERSUASION

Diplomacy.

GEMS, SEMI-PRECIOUS STONES, AND METALS

Emerald, aquamarine, peridot, jade, green zircon, green tourmaline, and alloys.

### Mercury-Type Celebrities

Babe Ruth, Ross Perot, Bill Gates, Brooke Shields, John Lennon, Harrison Ford.

THE BIRTH CHART OF BILL GATES

Mercury occupies its sign of exaltation (Virgo) in the 4th house along with Mars, and the Ascendant is in Gemini, whose ruler is Mercury. Let us recognize that the man is creative, intellectual, and has a business acumen that is the envy of everyone.

## Venus (*Shukra*) – "Harmony and synchronicity"

Acting as master of the demonic entities, Venus is shrouded in a thick atmosphere that traps the Sun's light very symmetrically while following the most circular orbit around the star of day. Venus shines

Natal chart — Bill Gates

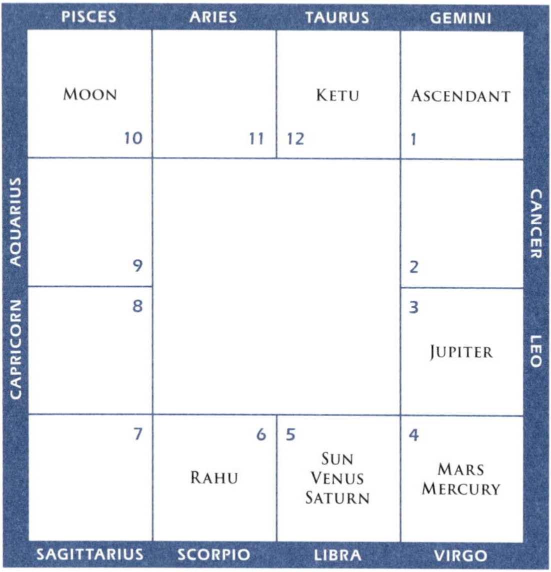


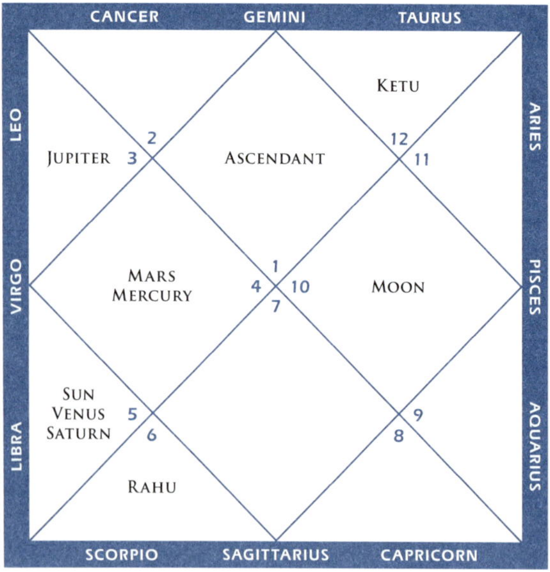

brightly and so is related to silver, diamonds, and all that is refined—like sugar, fine clothes, and other luxuries. Its high internal temperature indicates warmth and passion. Outwardly sweet and harmonious, it serves as a symbol of beauty and elegance, but may well have a deceptive side. As the proverb goes, "You can't always judge a book by its cover!"

People of the Venus type, the most beautiful and attractive of all, are very concerned about their appearance, which motivates them to avoid gaining weight. Their features are soft and their eyes, like their hair and skin, have a brilliant hue. Their nature is feminine and their sexual vitality strong. They have strength and endurance, coupled with a large reserve of vital energy, despite their apparent delicacy.

Somewhat vain and romantic, the failure of a relationship affects Venusians more than others. They hold the interests of society and other people close to their heart. They are very creative, as well as being great lovers of art in all its forms. Charm personified, the Venus type remains dedicated and loving, even though this may be hidden under his beautifully polished exterior.

In the charts of such individuals, Venus is dominant in the Ascendant or one of the three other quadrants, most ideally in Taurus, Libra, or Pisces, where it is exalted.

## Venus' Attributes

REPRESENTATIONS
Actors, artists, musicians, spouse, woman.

SIGNIFICATIONS

Comfort, vehicles, flowers, gems and jewellery, ornaments, arts.

POSITIVE ATTRIBUTES

Beauty, charm, affection, passion, friendship, love, kindness, sociability, balance, elegance, sophistication, grace, a cool and easygoing temperament, gentleness, developed aesthetic sense, sensitivity, diplomacy, the need for harmony, charm, sincerity, altruism, culture.

NEGATIVE ATTRIBUTES

Pride, sensual vice or corruption, indolence, selfishness, materialism, possessiveness, lack of charm, aesthetic sense, diplomacy, or culture, lust, vanity, frivolity.

FIELDS OF ACTION

Art, dance, theatre, cinema, music, mathematics, love relationships, and human relations in general.

OUTCOMES SOUGHT

Happiness, harmony, luxury, prosperity, wealth.

PHYSIOLOGY

Venus governs the kidneys, reproductive system, sensuality, desire, and sexual pleasure. It can also cause excess acidity. The Venusian is of medium height.

PREFERRED PLACES

Near rivers or other bodies of water, places of entertainment.

PREFERRED TIMES

Friday.

METHOD OF PERSUASION

Wise counsel.

GEMS, SEMI-PRECIOUS STONES, AND METALS.

Diamond, white sapphire, clear zircon, crystal, white coral, and silver.

### Venus-Type Celebrities

Bono, Queen Victoria, Charlie Chaplin, Elizabeth Taylor, Martha Stewart, Sidney Poitier.

THE BIRTH CHART OF BONO

The lead singer of the rock band U2 has a Libra Ascendant ruled by Venus with an aspect of Jupiter on the 1st house, which amplifies its qualities, while Venus is in Taurus, its own sign. As a songwriter, philanthropist, and charismatic leader of his group, Bono uses his creativity by playing various different roles. Besides, his voice is recognized as one of the sexiest in the rock music world.

## Mars (*Mangala*) – "Action!"

Mars, the red planet, is covered with canyons, rock dust, and towering volcanoes, and composed of oxides that corrode and break down the other elements. It has no atmosphere, although there once was water on its surface, which implies a kind of frustration and inability to nourish and comfort itself. The swirling dust storms symbolize anger, the high volcanoes spewing lava indicate the ability to exert the necessary effort to carry out desired actions, and the innumerable crevasses that crisscross the planet underlie a proneness to accidents, cuts, and burns of all kinds. Having once experienced the benefits of water, Mars still remains close to its emotions, except that its violent storms make its temperature rise quickly!

Mars represents the negative aspects of fire, and may predispose one to indigestion, an excess of bile and acidity, as well as overwarm blood that easily accumulates toxins. Acidic foods such as fried preparations, hot spices, meat, alcohol, and tobacco,

Natal chart — Bono

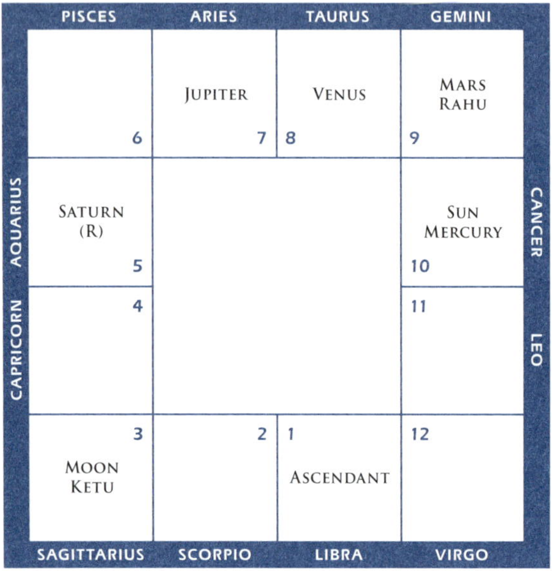


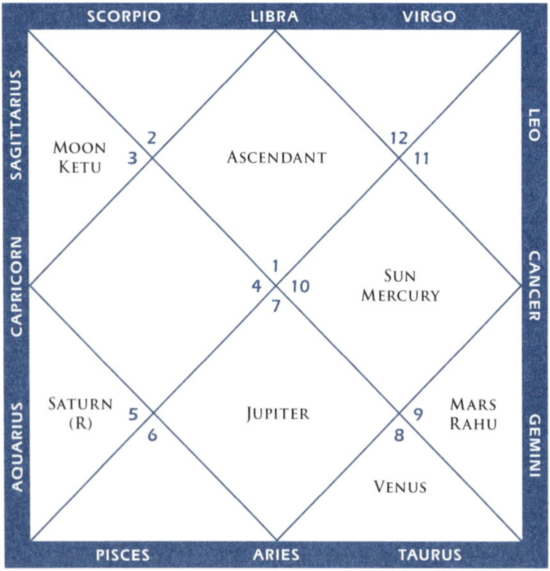

therefore do no good to the Martian type. Nevertheless, he is quite healthy, with angular features and a ruddy rather than pale complexion. His eyes are piercing, but sensitive to light and easily irritated.

Being very perceptive, the Martian type is critical, audacious, and quick to engage in debate. His strong logical faculties, however, can quickly give way to anger rather than a real sense of justice. He loves to win and proves to be a poor loser. Like a good commander, he demonstrates loyalty and favours alliances to confront his opponents. Good with his hands, he also often excels in the technical or scientific domains.

In the charts of such individuals, Mars is dominant in the Ascendant or one of the three other quadrants, especially in Aries or Scorpio, or exalted in Capricorn and in the company of naturally benefic planets.

## Mars' Attributes

#### REPRESENTATIONS

Builders, managers, designers, engineers, policemen, soldiers, enemies, brothers, and sisters.

#### SIGNIFICATIONS

Agitation, violence, resentment, accidents, arguments, battles, surgery, war, fire.

#### POSITIVE ATTRIBUTES

Athleticism, determination, ability to satisfy one's desires, courage, ambition, heroism, audacity, moral and muscular strength, passion, action, focused energy, competitive spirit, an "all or nothing" attitude, a domineering and resolute spirit, energy, endurance, organizational skill, practicality, independence, resourcefulness, deep and penetrating intelligence, zeal, leadership qualities.

NEGATIVE ATTRIBUTES

Bitterness, hostility, anger, hastiness, obstinacy, inconsistency, a taste for provocation and strife, violence, cruelty, brutality, impulsiveness, lack of control, recklessness, selfishness, tyranny, destructiveness, sadomasochism, perversion, jealousy, lack of motivation, indifference, laziness.

FIELDS OF ACTION

Computer work, heroic acts, construction, firearms, real estate, mining and metalwork, exploiting others' passions, protection, sports.

OUTCOMES SOUGHT

The experience of the dynamism and rhythm of life in actions and interactions.

PHYSIOLOGY

Mars regulates bile, bone marrow, blood, muscle, sex, burns, cuts, and other injuries. The Martian type is physically on the short side.

PREFERRED PLACES

Near fire.

PREFERRED TIMES

Day and night, Tuesday.

METHOD OF PERSUASION

Punishment.

GEMS, SEMI-PRECIOUS STONES, AND METALS

Red coral, carnelian, red jasper, and copper.

## Mars-Type Celebrities

Adolph Hitler, Martin Luther King, Muhammad Ali, Christopher Reeve, Bruce Lee, Nietzsche, Gérard Depardieu, Marquis de Sade, O. J. Simpson.

Natal chart — Adolf Hitler

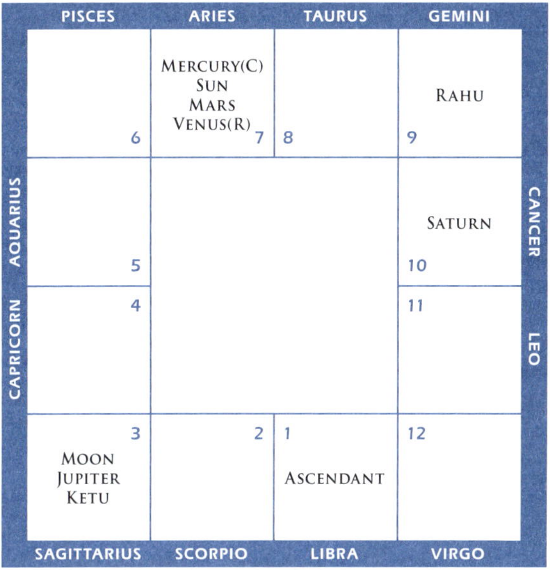


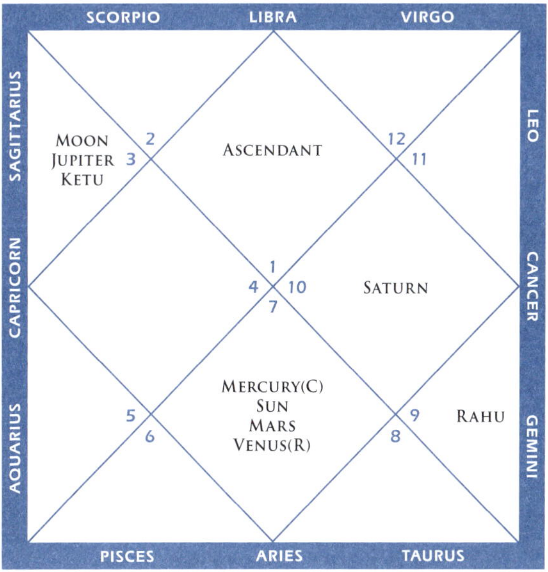

THE BIRTH CHART OF ADOLPH HITLER

Mars occupies its own sign in the 7th house. The Sun, also in Aries, is in its sign of exaltation. Everyone knows the story and exploits of this dominant Martian type.

## Jupiter (*Guru*) – "Expanding consciousness"

Jupiter, the largest of the planets that orbit the Sun, is the spiritual master of the gods. It generates more heat than it receives from the Sun. Many moons of all kinds—gaseous, earth-like, etc.—orbit around it like students around their teacher. Not hot enough to become a star, Jupiter is still very radiant and promotes growth and expansion, great ideas, philosophy, and spirituality. Whereas Mercury, another knowledge planet, makes use of discriminative power, Jupiter exudes a knowledge matured by meditative study.

People of the Jupiter type, whose complexion is on the golden side, usually have good muscles, but are also a bit fleshy, which may lead to excess weight with age. Physically strong, Jupiterians love the outdoors and exercise. Their most vulnerable organs are the pancreas, spleen, and liver, so it is advisable for them to go easy on oily, fried, and sweet foods. Joyful and naturally fulfilled, they love being with people in general, but especially with their own circle of friends and family. They are enthusiastic, expressive, and optimistic, but might go to excess in the company of Venus or Rahu. Anything related to education, business, banking, management, and law fits them like a glove. Empathetic and dedicated, idealistic Jupiterians might also take interest in philosophy, music, justice, and all forms of ritual.

In the natal charts of such individuals, Jupiter is dominant in the Ascendant or one of the three other quadrants, or in a trine (houses 5 or 9), preferably in Sagittarius, Pisces, or Cancer—its exaltation sign—and in the company of the Moon.

## Jupiter's Attributes

### REPRESENTATIONS

Bankers, children, foreigners, idea makers, judges, lawyers, teachers, ministers.

### SIGNIFICATIONS

Truth, money, mantras, philosophy, pilgrimage, religion and spirituality, sacred texts, seeking what is best.

### POSITIVE ATTRIBUTES

Benevolence, compassion, devotion, morality, optimism, virtue, progress and development, humanism, generosity, cheerfulness and humour, genius, common sense, synthetic and coherent thinking, wisdom, tolerance, rectitude, loyalty, philosophical spirit, respect for law and tradition, favoured by life.

### NEGATIVE ATTRIBUTES

Inflated ego, greed, extravagance, immorality, excessive sensuality, megalomania, fanaticism, bigotry, intolerance, partiality, hypocrisy, dishonesty, attachment to comfort, insatiable greed, carelessness, confusion, anarchy, rebellion, false beliefs.

### FIELDS OF ACTION

Astrology, meditation, charity, justice, law and legal affairs, faith, speculation, education, games of chance.

### OUTCOMES SOUGHT

Wealth, happiness, knowledge, luck, prosperity, wisdom.

PHYSIOLOGY

Jupiter governs the adipose tissue, liver, hips, abdomen, and allergies.

PREFERRED PLACES

The sky and the Northeast.

PREFERRED TIMES

Thursday and long trips.

METHOD OF PERSUASION

Wise counsel.

GEMS, SEMI-PRECIOUS STONES, AND METALS

Yellow sapphire, yellow topaz, citrine, yellow zircon, yellow tourmaline, and gold-plated tin.

### Jupiter-Type Celebrities

The Dalai Lama, Paul Newman, Bill Cosby, Ben Affleck, Bhagwan Shree Rajneesh, Mikhail Gorbachev.

THE BIRTH CHART OF PAUL NEWMAN

His Ascendant is in Sagittarius, where there are three benefics including Jupiter in its own sign. His life and success as an actor, director, producer, screenwriter, racing driver, entrepreneur, and philanthropist are a testimony to the expansiveness and good fortune associated with Jupiter.

## Saturn (*Shani*) – "Awareness of time and space"

Saturn, the coldest, most gaseous, most remote, and slowest of the planets taken into account in Vedic astrology, embodies the notion of exile, prison, hospital, and faraway places. Its coldness is reminiscent of death,

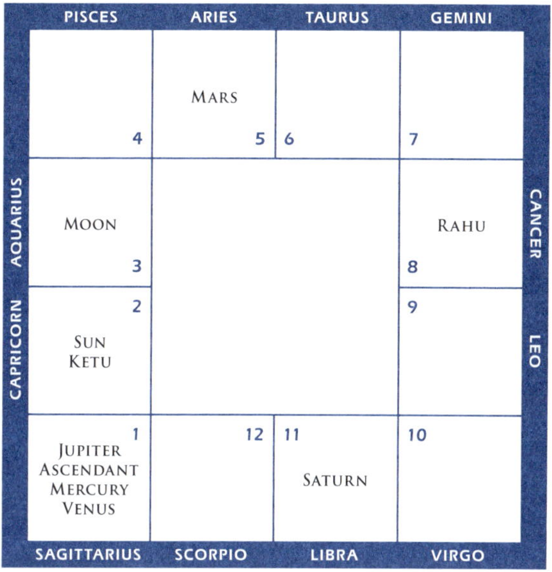


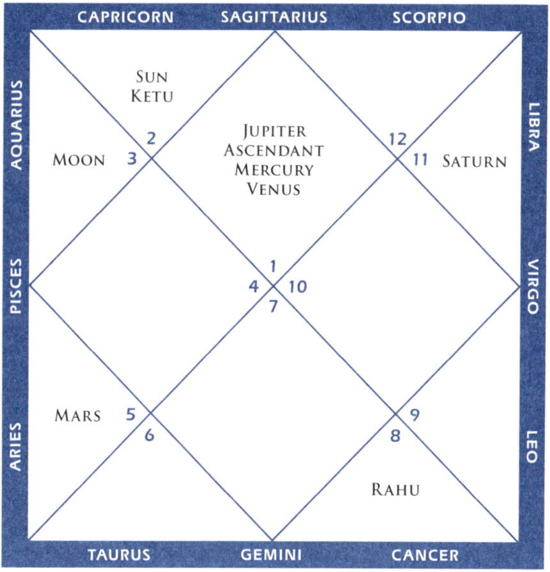


Natal chart — Paul Newman

ignorance of the principles of life, and destruction; it creates lamentation and incites to renunciation. Its blackness diminishes one's clarity of mind and promotes a rigid realism, even pessimism. The rings of ice and debris surrounding it are indicative of its association with anything that is dirty or old and, as it lies on the very borders of our solar system, it evokes boundaries to be transgressed. Its rotation on itself is very fast, a guarantee of hard and steady work, but progress made under its influence is durable. Structure, discipline, and accountability are the watchwords here.

Physically, the Saturnian type is considered the least attractive of all. He is often characterized by dry, chapped, cracked, and mottled brown skin, with brittle nails and hair. As his digestion is rather slow and difficult and his circulation poor, he often loses vitality and endurance. Serious and pragmatic, Saturnians tend to see life in black and white and to succumb to depression. Introverted by nature, they can become selfish and insensitive to the problems of others.

Fortunately, Saturn is not the only planet in our solar system, and its influence is often modified by its sisters, who can turn the Saturnian type into an artist, a philosopher, or a dedicated worker. In its highest expression, Saturn produces yogis, monks, and spiritualists who renounce the pleasures of this world to seek spiritual perfection. Conversely, there will be criminals, tyrants, and people trapped in their egos and obsessed by their bodily needs. Saturn is a planet to monitor closely, because we all have it in our chart!

In the charts of such individuals, Saturn is dominant in the Ascendant or in one of the three other quadrants, especially in Capricorn, Aquarius, or Libra, where it is exalted. Saturn should best avoid Mars and Rahu, while it is benefited by the company of Jupiter and Venus.

## Saturn's Attributes

### REPRESENTATIONS

Authority figures, the elderly, hermits, monks, servants, Shiva.

### SIGNIFICATIONS

Sense of responsibility, restrictions, fear, death, loss of vitality, isolation, separation, guilt, illness, adversity, denial, poverty, obstructions, accidents, spirituality, sacred texts, minerals, penalties, and misfortune.

### POSITIVE ATTRIBUTES

Ambition, asceticism, discipline, humility, honesty, detachment, persistence, reliability, realism, coherence, solitude, resignation, responsibility, sincerity, conservatism, sense of effort and duty, strength, endurance, firmness and internal stability, reserve, prudence, meditation, method, rigor, loyalty, idealism, advocacy.

### NEGATIVE ATTRIBUTES

Laziness, anxiety, rigidity, melancholy, suspicion, coldness, isolation, misanthropy, paranoia, introversion, self-contempt, lack of concentration, slowness, sectarianism, greed, hypocrisy, cruelty, evasion of responsibility, workaholism.

### FIELDS OF ACTION

Agriculture, construction, conservation, mining, philosophy.

### OUTCOMES SOUGHT

Wisdom and detachment.

PHYSIOLOGY

Saturn governs chronic diseases, death, longevity, depression, fear, remorse, concentration, joints, nervous tissue, and paralysis. The Saturnian type is tall.

PREFERRED PLACES

Mines, earthy and dirty places.

PREFERRED TIMES

Saturday and extra time.

METHOD OF PERSUASION

Diplomacy.

GEMS, SEMI-PRECIOUS STONES, AND METALS

Blue sapphire, lapis lazuli, amethyst, turquoise, blue zircon, blue tourmaline, iron, steel, coal.

### Saturn-Type Celebrities

Barack Obama, Abraham Lincoln, Karl Marx, Goethe, Charles Manson, Jimmy Carter.

THE BIRTH CHART OF ABRAHAM LINCOLN

A positive Saturnian par excellence. The Ascendant, Sun, and Moon—very personal elements in a chart—all occupy the signs of Saturn, namely Capricorn and Aquarius with Saturn in evidence in a quadrant. In the service of his country and all its citizens, and despite conflicts and war, this U.S. president firmly guided the ship of state in order to achieve equality for all.

## The Lunar Nodes

It was mentioned earlier that the ascending and descending nodes of the Moon correspond to the

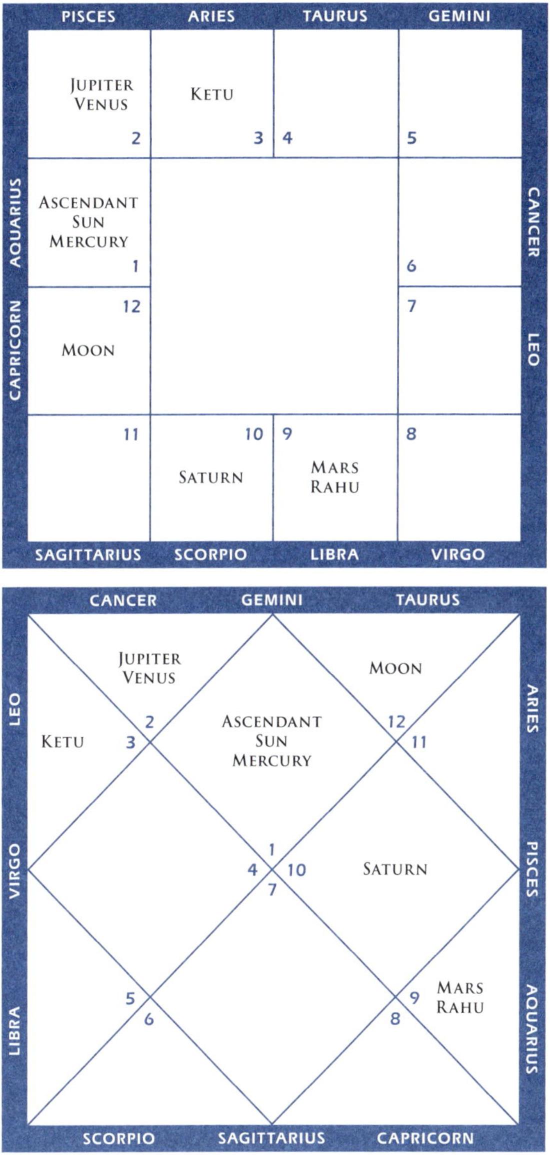


Natal chart — Abraham Lincoln

intersection points of the Moon's orbit with the ecliptic, and have no gross physical form of their own. Because of this, Rahu and Ketu are sometimes called phantom planets, with all the mystery such a name evokes. To better understand their role, let us hear the story of their origin from Indian mythology.

Millions of years ago, the gods joined with the demonic entities in an effort to extract the nectar of immortality from the ocean of milk by churning it. During this process, an enormous amount of poison was at first generated, making it necessary for Lord Shiva to intervene and save everyone by drinking the poison. Though he remained otherwise unharmed, the poison turned his throat blue, and all representations of Shiva to this day show him with this memento of his heroic deed.

The gods and demons resumed their efforts, and after some time, the nectar they desired appeared. The demons wanted to seize it immediately, but Vishnu, disguised as an enchanting beauty, intervened and offered to distribute a fair share of the nectar to both sides. The seductress began by serving the gods, all the while smiling and charmingly fluttering her eyelashes at the demons who were so completely captivated that they immediately forgot all about the nectar.

Only one of them, Rahu, who was more perceptive than the others, could see that they were being tricked and realized that the nectar would all run out before the alluring beauty got around to the demons, so he cunningly slipped in between the gods and took a place in line. He barely had time to swallow his share of the elixir of immortality before the Sun and the Moon recognized him and denounced him to Vishnu who, on the spot, severed his head from his body by a stroke of his swift lightning-like discus. Having swallowed the nectar, Rahu could not die; instead, he at once became two entities, Rahu and Ketu, the eternal enemies of the Sun and the Moon.

Therefore, from the astronomical point of view, whenever the Sun and the Moon come too close to the ascending and descending nodes, an eclipse takes place, and the approaching luminary becomes temporarily shrouded in darkness. Thus, by their intelligence, Rahu and Ketu can also dominate other planets. Let's take a closer look.

### *Rahu* (Moon's Ascending Node) – "Appearances first and foremost"

The Rahu type has a mysterious and unpredictable way about him, making him difficult to understand. He can simultaneously attract and disturb others, as he combines features of both Saturn and Venus at the same time, which lends him a kind of black beauty that is quite unusual.

Generally thin, people of the Rahu type have a sensitive digestive system, like Saturnian types. They are rather nervous, their movements are executed with speed, and their weak immune system exposes them to contagious diseases. Even though Rahu is not considered to belong to any particular social group in the hierarchy of planets, it still gives the people of its type intelligence, intuition, and creativity, but in unconventional ways. The mass media are of the Rahu type, and those under its influence work better with foreigners or abroad. They are ambitious and rarely satisfied with their accomplishments, which may cause them considerable psychological distress. Somewhat weak in constitution, these people may be victims of possession by other entities, and bear the brunt of unfulfilled desires or curses.

In the charts of such individuals, Rahu occupies a dominant position in the Ascendant or one of the three other quadrants, or in houses 3, 6, or 11, often accompanied by the Moon or the Sun. The favourable position of the lord of the sign in which Rahu is situated is also a factor.

## Rahu's Attributes

REPRESENTATIONS
Rodents, reptiles, and insects.

SIGNIFICATIONS
Fears and phobias, extraversion, megalomania, compulsiveness, disappointments, complications, psychology, entanglement, adversity, material benefits, minerals, drugs, poisons and toxins, madness.

POSITIVE ATTRIBUTES
Originality, individuality, independence, determination, courage, ambition, magnetism, exceptional talent, insight, ingenuity, inspiration, imagination, thirst for expansion and power, insatiable material desires.

NEGATIVE ATTRIBUTES
Confusion, escapism, neurosis, psychosis, addiction, illusion, laziness, ignorance, indolence, separation, eccentricity, explosive temperament.

FIELDS OF ACTION
Crime, fraud, science, intellect, esoterism.

OUTCOMES SOUGHT

Irregular and difficult to predict.

PHYSIOLOGY

Rahu controls the legs, spleen, nervous system, and chronic conditions. The Rahu type is generally tall.

GEMS, SEMI-PRECIOUS STONES, AND METALS

Garnet, honey-coloured agate, lead.

### Rahu-Type Celebrities

Prince, Stacey Wolf, Tony Curtis, Christina Ricci, Brian Keith, Michael Landon, Mick Jagger.

THE BIRTH CHART OF PRINCE

Rahu is in the Ascendant, in the sign of Libra, with Venus in Aries, an aspect that bestows on him strength and power in the arts. As a self-taught multi-instrumentalist, Prince has had a very prolific career as a producer, composer, singer, and musician of American pop and funk. He can play more than twenty instruments and records his albums entirely alone, though he knows neither how to read nor write music. His physical appearance is also characteristic of the Rahu type.

## *Ketu* (Moon's Descending Node) – "Introspection and detachment"

The Ketu type resembles the Martian type. His musculature is less developed, which makes him tend to be thin, and his rapid metabolism makes him susceptible to various blood disorders. Even though lean and wiry, his eyes are piercing and quite distinctive. He may suffer from neuromuscular disorders or lack of

Natal chart — Prince

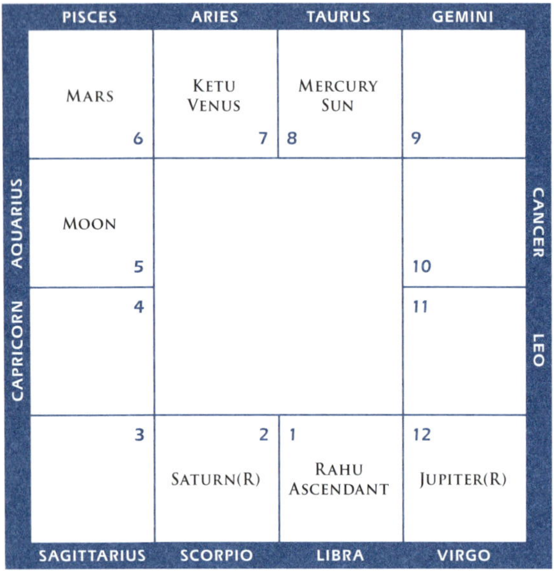


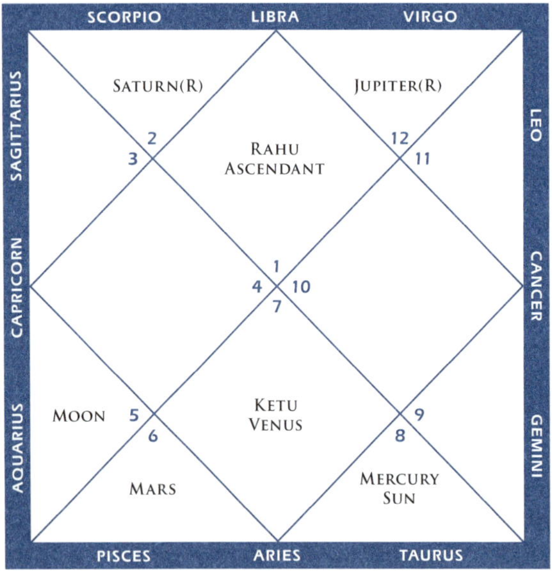

coordination, and be prone to accidents at public events or injury from natural disasters.

People of the Ketu type are independent thinkers who may even be obsessive, and can be quite introverted and eccentric, sometimes to the point of insensitivity. Intolerant of criticism, they react strongly because of a self-doubt that may even lead to a tendency for self-destruction.

Ketu types make good soldiers, scientists, or mathematicians, and excel at the computer. Their powers of concentration, discrimination, and scrutiny lead them into a world where they forget everything else. They may also become astrologers, physicians, or persons possessing occult or spiritual knowledge. When they are more evolved, Ketu types see the temporary and illusory nature of worldly things in spite of external circumstances.

In the charts of such individuals, Ketu occupies a dominant position in the Ascendant or one of the three other quadrants, or in the 12th house, with which he has a natural affinity, preferably in conjunction with the Moon or the Sun.

### KETU'S ATTRIBUTES

#### REPRESENTATIONS

Maternal grandmother and grandfather, ghosts, reptiles, and insects.

#### SIGNIFICATIONS

Loss, introversion, personal fantasies, science fiction, illusion and evasion of problems, astral forces, dreams, enlightenment or liberation, electricity, the Internet, accidents, sleep, therapeutical diets, natural healing techniques.

POSITIVE ATTRIBUTES

Asceticism, individualism, detachment from the pleasures of this world, psychic gifts, universalism, compassion, impressionability, idealism, intuition, self-sacrifice, subtlety, ambition, spirituality, penetrating mind, artistry, charm, unconventionality.

NEGATIVE ATTRIBUTES

Eccentric and explosive temper, selfishness, anti-sociability, vindictiveness, fanaticism and bigotry, imbalance, violence, confusion, hypersensitivity, cheating, emotional tension, impulsiveness, amorality.

FIELDS OF ACTION

Surgery, military life, clairvoyance, astrology, healing, monastic life, detective, spy, artist.

OUTCOMES SOUGHT

Irregular and difficult to predict.

PHYSIOLOGY

Ketu governs the nails, breath, stomach, spleen, and diseases that are difficult to diagnose. The Ketu type is tall.

GEMS, SEMI-PRECIOUS STONES, AND METALS

Cat's-eye, tiger's-eye, chrysoberyl.

## Ketu-Type Celebrities

Donald Trump, Angelina Jolie, Kevin Kline, George Clooney, John Travolta.

THE BIRTH CHART OF ANGELINA JOLIE

Ketu is in Taurus with the Sun and Mercury, while Venus, the ruler of Taurus, is in the Ascendant, thus enhancing the influence of Taurus. Everyone recognizes

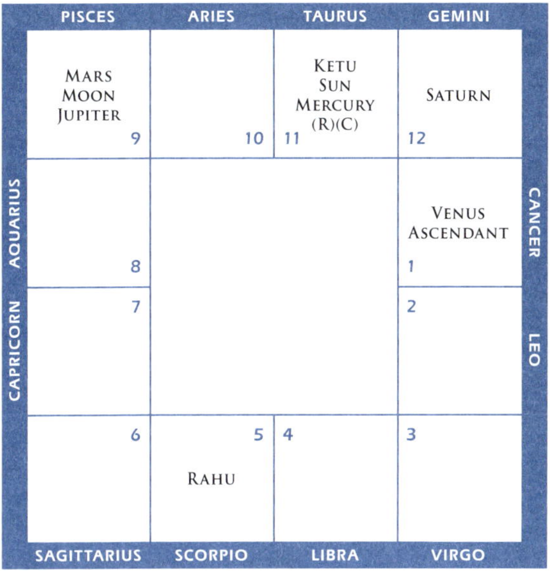


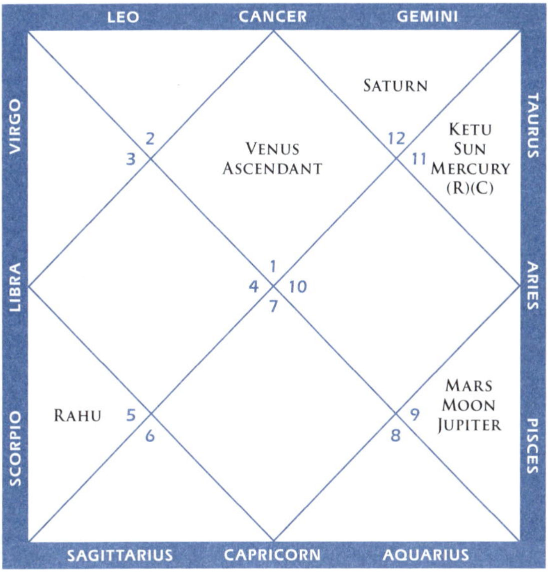


Natal chart — Angelina Jolie

that her eyes are among her most remarkable physical assets, not to mention her slender form. As a child, Angelina collected snakes and lizards, and at 14, she wanted to become a funeral director—can't get much more eccentric than that! She then adopted a lifestyle marked by excess, wearing only black and dyeing her hair purple. Even today, she insists that in her heart, she is always just "a little punk with tattoos."

## Exercise 1 – Exploring a Chart

Enough work, time to play! Take out your own chart to try and apply the principles of interpretation while we examine that of a mystery dancer, singer, and songwriter from the United States. Can you guess who it is?

As we go along, we will keep adding new elements, so that you will learn about their influence and importance. But since we have only covered the planets up till now, let us begin by examining the relations that exist between them.

### The Influence of the Planets on Our Mystery Star

The Moon here is in conjunction with Ketu and Venus, in opposition to Rahu. We also have a Sun-Mercury conjunction aspected by Saturn without being altogether in opposition, while also receiving aspects by Mars and Rahu.

#### MOON • KETU • VENUS

The "introspective and detached" Ketu is here in conjunction with the Moon, i.e., "unconditional love." This combination of Ketu and the Moon is known to

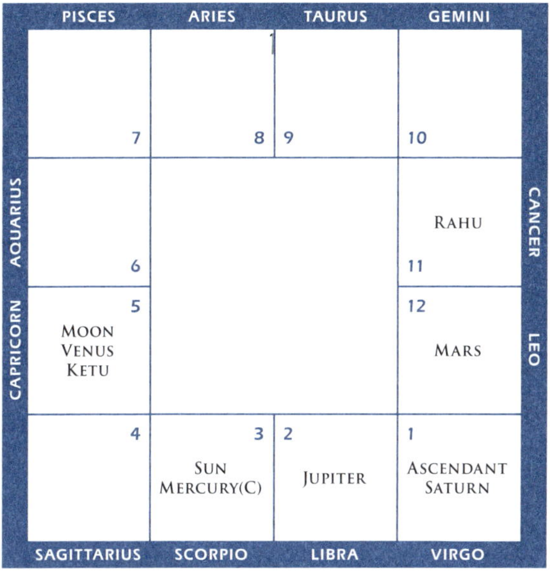
PISCES
ARIES
TAURUS
GEMINI
7
8
9
10
AQUARIUS
6
RAHU
11
CANCER
CAPRICORN
5
MOON
VENUS
KETU
12
MARS
LEO
4
3
SUN
MERCURY(C)
2
JUPITER
1
ASCENDANT
SATURN
SAGITTARIUS
SCORPIO
LIBRA
VIRGO

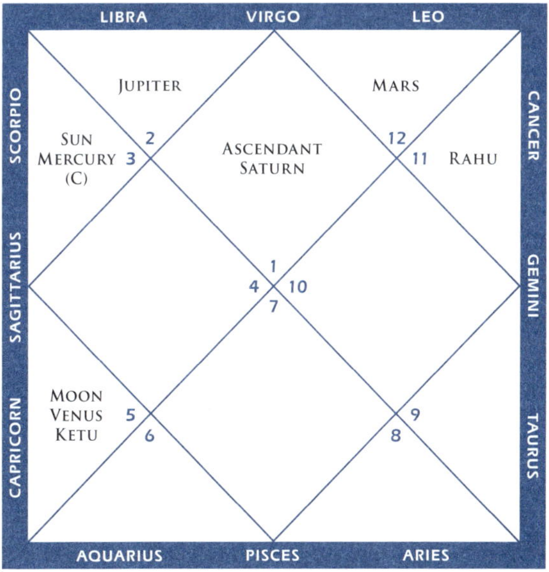
LIBRA
VIRGO
LEO
SCORPIO
JUPITER
MARS
CANCER
SUN
MERCURY
(C)
2
3
ASCENDANT
SATURN
12
11
RAHU
SAGITTARIUS
1
4
10
7
GEMINI
CAPRICORN
MOON
VENUS
KETU
5
6
9
8
TAURUS
AQUARIUS
PISCES
ARIES

produce a person who seeks to depart from normality or the banal, who "floats" on a different plane. This might result in psychological problems or a desire to liberate oneself from all that is needed for physical survival. In extreme cases, we could speak of a hunger for transcendence. This combination might also indicate a tendency to be swayed by the environment to the extent that one's identity is confused with one's environment and the people in it.

Ketu's influence may also be seen in connection with the various indicators and persons connected with the Moon, especially the mother, the masses, and early childhood. As Ketu also represents the Internet, this native might influence the masses through this media (in fact, she has for several years been statistically the most sought after personality on the Internet).

In this threesome, the beneficial Venus—"harmony and synchronicity"—though less lavish in her kindness than the bountiful Jupiter, ensures a great appearance and attractive features beautifying the Moon which represents the face. The Moon's influence also confers an emotional and imaginative nature (Fairy godmothers at work!). This combination also reveals a certain detachment, separations, and other "surprises" in those areas normally ruled by Venus, such as personal relationships, especially with the life partner.

As Venus is superficial in nature, we can discern here a kind of fraud, a tendency to deceive, and a lack of stability in love. Although the Moon, which represents the mind and emotions, is here in conjunction with Venus, the planet of the arts, it is also afflicted by Rahu and Ketu, who bring confusion, unpredictability, and a desire to escape reality, mainly with the help of intoxicating substances. By checking the degrees of the planets, we find that Ketu and Venus are closely conjoined at the same degree, which is good for Ketu, but not for Venus, whose attributes are completely overwhelmed by the lunar nodes.

### SUN • MERCURY

This combination is considered to be a source of intelligence, which is not at all affected by Mercury's combustion at 5 degrees from the Sun. Everything would be fine if it were not for the three malefic aspects (Rahu, Mars, and Saturn). What can we deduce from that?

Given that the father figure is represented by the Sun, we can infer that the father of this native is at least a controlling or confrontational character, if he is not absent altogether. And since the Sun also stands for self-esteem, this configuration may indicate a lack of it in our subject.

The three malefic aspects noted above will also bring out the negative attributes of Mercury, most notably a kind of discrimination favouring instability, lying, eccentricity, or even perversity.

### MARS

We note that Mars, which is here the "soul significator," is sandwiched between two malefics, Rahu and Saturn, in the neighbouring houses. Their presence creates a

Table of degrees — Mystery star

| | | | | | |
|---|---|---|---|---|---|
| Ascendant | 9°47′ | Mercury | 16°26′ | Rahu | 1°09′ |
| Saturn | 25°40′ | Ketu | 1°09′ | Mars | 29°40′ |
| Jupiter | 7°24′ | Venus | 1°30′ | | |
| Sun | 11°49′ | Moon | 18°47′ | | |

kind of prison for Mars, so that our native must feel oppressed and deprived of freedom. We may suspect that during the maturation of Mars, this person will particularly suffer from this planetary alignment. The Sun's and Mercury's years of maturation might also prove painful.

This chart has no exalted or retrograde planets.

## Tips for Exploring Your Own Chart

And now, as for you, what are the aspects, conjunctions, and oppositions in your chart? Do you have any planets in exaltation or debilitation? What is your ruling planet, i.e., your soul significator?

If one of your planets benefits from the conjunction or aspect of several benefic planets—particularly in the absence of malefic interventions—you will find that the significations of this planet will be particularly positive in your life.

If your Moon is conjoined with the Sun, you were born on the day of the new Moon. In this case, you probably find your life more difficult than you'd like, since this combination often gives a sense of being victimized.

Saturn in conjunction with the Moon may indicate a depressive tendency, and in contact with the Sun can undermine self-esteem, whereas if these two planets are in opposition, the result may be some difficulty with authority figures, unless it means that you were deprived of the happiness of an unbroken family in childhood.

Through contact with the Moon, Mars can make one's behaviour more aggressive or harm one's relationship with the mother, whereas in conjunction with the Sun, it often indicates a distance, real or felt, from the father figure.

This is the way the planets exert their influence on each other.

Now, let's take a closer look at the signs.

# Chapter 2

# THE SIGNS OF THE ZODIAC

## The Signs

Each of the 12 signs of the zodiac covers 30 degrees and represents a part of the body of the Cosmic Man who personifies Time. Together, they form the background on which the planets move in their course across the sky, and on which they exert their influence.

| Symbol | Sign | Lord of the Sign | Corresponding House |
|---|---|---|---|
| ♈ | Aries (Mesha) | Mars | 1 |
| ♉ | Taurus (Vrishaba) | Venus | 2 |
| ♊ | Gemini (Mithuna) | Mercury | 3 |
| ♋ | Cancer (Kataka) | Moon | 4 |
| ♌ | Leo (Simha) | Sun | 5 |
| ♍ | Virgo (Kanya) | Mercury | 6 |
| ♎ | Libra (Thula) | Venus | 7 |
| ♏ | Scorpio (Vrishika) | Mars | 8 |
| ♐ | Sagittarius (Dhanus) | Jupiter | 9 |
| ♑ | Capricorn (Makara) | Saturn | 10 |
| ♒ | Aquarius (Kumbha) | Saturn | 11 |
| ♓ | Pisces (Mina) | Jupiter | 12 |

Each sign also influences its corresponding house. For example, the first house will always have some of Aries' characteristics, even if, in a specific chart, it is actually in Gemini or some other sign. The houses thus inherit a portion of the influence of the sign with which they are traditionally associated, in addition to being affected by the sign in which they are found.

As all the signs are related to body parts, this comes in handy to help us assess the effects of the planets. For example, a powerful Jupiter in Cancer might give a larger chest compared to the family average of a person. Similarly, Venus would make the body part of the sign hosting it beautiful whereas Saturn will give slenderness. And the same applies to the houses described in the next chapter.

## The Lord of the Sign

From the previous table, we can see that each sign is governed by a "lord" or "ruler" who also becomes the "dispositor" of any planets found in its sign(s). This is an important factor, since a planet, even if exalted, cannot fully manifest its qualities if its dispositor is, for example, in a state of fall or debilitation.

## The Characteristics of the Signs

The table found on pages 92-93 summarizes the characteristics of each sign.

### Preferred Times

- **Day signs** are generally more open in nature. People under the influence of these signs often find the first part of their life more fruitful than the latter.

- **Night signs** are more secretive, and those marked by them generally do better in the second half of their life than the first.

## Modes

- **The movable mode** is linked to movement, change, and dynamism. For instance, if Saturn is in a movable sign, the sense of responsibility it confers will be expressed more actively.

- **The fixed mode** favours stability and conservatism, even stasis. Saturn in fixed signs would make its sense of responsibility virtually unshakable and produce lasting results. The karma associated with the fixed signs is also more difficult to change.

- **The dual mode** combines the results of the movable and fixed modes, which can provide stability in change, or flexibility and adaptability in a life of routine. Saturn in a dual sign might be more flexible where responsibilities are concerned, but at the same time be indecisive, vacillating, or even confused.

## Elements

- **Fire** represents people who are active, intense, quick-witted, and slender in body.

| Symbol | Sign | Body Parts | Time |
|---|---|---|---|
| ♈ | Aries | Head | Night |
| ♉ | Taurus | Face and Neck | Night |
| ♊ | Gemini | Shoulders and arms | Night |
| ♋ | Cancer | Chest and heart | Night |
| ♌ | Leo | Stomach | Day |
| ♍ | Virgo | Upper abdomen | Day |
| ♎ | Libra | Lower abdomen | Day |
| ♏ | Scorpio | Genitalia | Day |
| ♐ | Sagittarius | Hips and thighs | Night |
| ♑ | Capricorn | Knees | Night |
| ♒ | Aquarius | Legs and ankles | Day |
| ♓ | Pisces | Feet | Day |

If very intense, fire can even confer dominance. Where the body is concerned, such persons are assured of having a good digestion.

- **Air** indicates people who like change while being sensitive, sometimes to the point of being easily disturbed and irritated. Enterprising, focused on travel, they can be quite charitable.

| Mode | Element | Polarity | Gender |
|---|---|---|---|
| Movable | Fire | Positive | Male |
| Fixed | Earth | Negative | Female |
| Dual | Air | Positive | Male |
| Movable | Water | Negative | Female |
| Fixed | Fire | Positive | Male |
| Dual | Earth | Negative | Female |
| Movable | Air | Positive | Male |
| Fixed | Water | Negative | Female |
| Dual | Fire | Positive | Male |
| Movable | Earth | Negative | Female |
| Fixed | Air | Positive | Male |
| Dual | Water | Negative | Female |

- **Earth** produces people at ease in the realm of matter, who are particularly suited to enjoy good food, perfumes, and comfort. Their carefree nature also helps them to easily forgive or forget.

- **Water** only briefly retains the impressions that touch it, so that those dominated by this element do not suffer the stresses caused by their environment as much as others do. Their natural disposition for harmony and kindness leads them more often than not to experience a rewarding social life.

### Polarity

- **Positive**: Produces assertive, determined, and courageous people. Active, vigorous, and dynamic, they are self-confident.

- **Negative**: People under the influence of such signs internalize their energy and are receptive to others. Sensitive, sweet, and secretive, they tend to be vulnerable and impressionable, but also conciliatory and diplomatic.

### Gender

- **Masculine**: The odd signs, which make one more dynamic, aggressive, and assertive.

- **Female**: The even signs, which make one more gentle and receptive, tending to be supportive of others.

### In Chart Format

The following chart, as per the South Indian layout, will help you grasp the subtleties behind the combination of the various characteristics inherent to each sign:

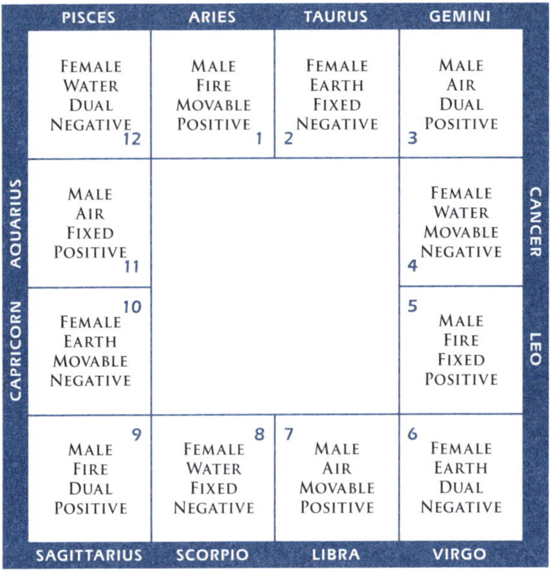


The characteristics of the signs

## Aspects Between Signs

As eager and attentive readers, you will no doubt recall that the planets "look" or aspect various points of the horoscope. Well, you'll be delighted to discover that the signs do the same thing! A distinction exists, however, between the aspects of the planets and those of the signs. We could say that the planets direct an intention towards the elements they aspect, while signs exercise a direct influence.

Here are the signs that each sign aspects:

- Aries: Leo, Scorpio, Aquarius (fixed signs)
- Taurus: Cancer, Libra, Capricorn (movable signs)

Aspects of the movable and fixed signs

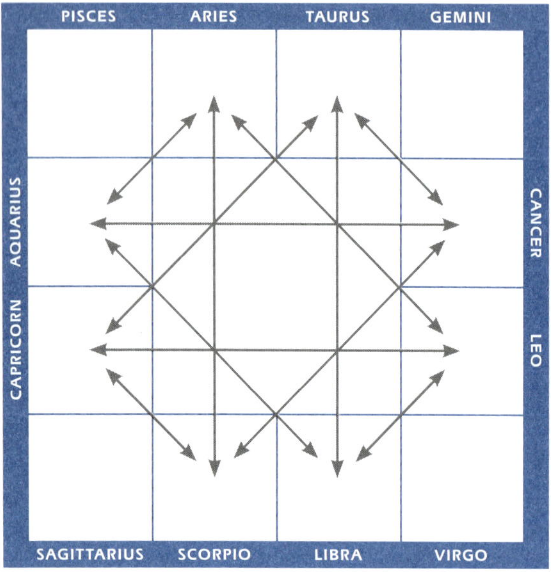


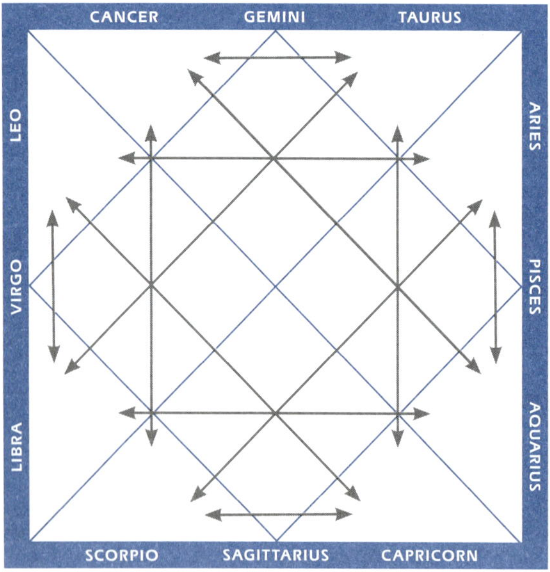

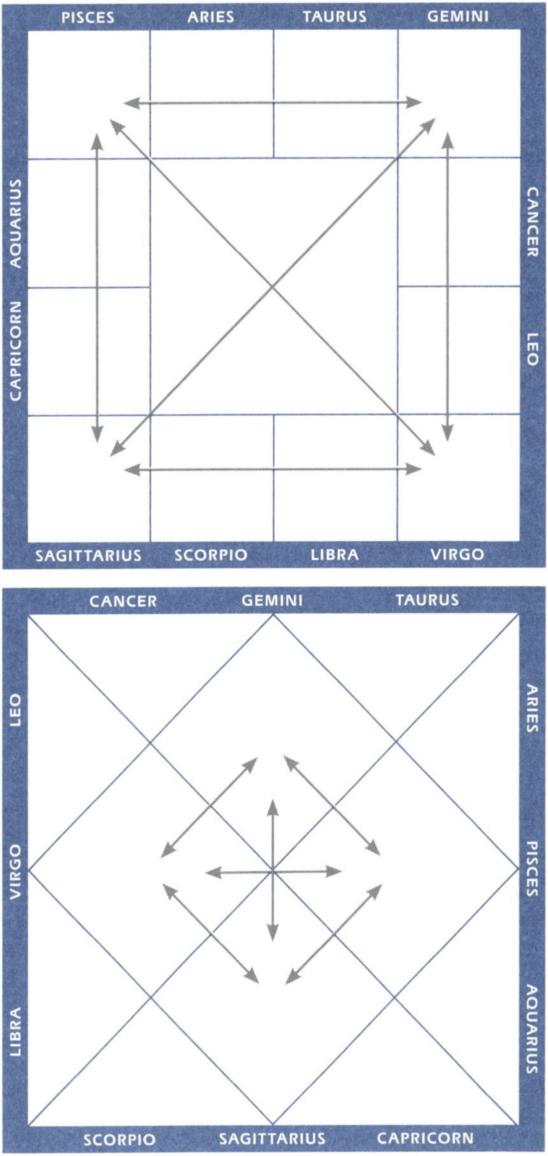


Aspects of the dual signs

- ❖ Gemini : Virgo, Sagittarius, Pisces (dual signs)
- ❖ Cancer: Taurus, Scorpio, Aquarius
- ❖ Leo: Aries, Libra, Capricorn
- ❖ Virgo : Sagittarius, Pisces, Gemini
- ❖ Libra: Aquarius, Taurus, Leo
- ❖ Scorpio: Capricorn, Aries, Cancer
- ❖ Sagittarius: Pisces, Gemini, Virgo
- ❖ Capricorn: Taurus, Leo, Scorpio
- ❖ Aquarius: Aries, Cancer, Libra
- ❖ Pisces: Gemini, Virgo, Sagittarius

All the movable signs aspect the fixed signs, except for those in their immediate neighbourhood (e.g., Aries does not aspect Taurus).

All fixed signs aspect the movable signs, except for those in their immediate neighbourhood (e.g., Taurus does not aspect Aries, nor Leo Cancer).

All dual signs aspect the other dual signs.

The diagrams on pages 96-97 illustrate the aspects exchanged by the signs.

## Key Significations of the Signs

We have already talked about significators in the chapter on the planets. Like the planets, the signs of the zodiac are also significators. For example, Libra is the significator of business relationships, and Cancer of mother and home. Therefore, if Venus is in Libra and both planet and sign receive only favourable aspects, we can conclude that the native's business relationships are harmonious and productive. Similarly, a Moon nicely aspected in Cancer is a good indicator of having a loving mother and a peaceful home.

An examination of the attributes of each sign will help us better understand the influence of the modes, elements, polarities, and genders. These characteristics reveal the proper way to read each sign, whether it is Aries, who must act at any cost, even at the risk of breaking his neck, or Taurus, who works, but in such a mechanical fashion that even he is likely to find himself boring!

## The Ascendant

The zodiac sign that is rising on the eastern horizon at the moment of birth is called the Ascendant. This sign is a uniquely important element in the chart, and it particularly affects one's physical constitution, behaviour, and personality.

### ♈ Aries

- **Physical features**: average height, lean and muscular, athletic, strong frame, curly hair.
- **Significations**: action, authority, accidents, struggle.

- **Strengths**: courage, initiative, autonomy, assertiveness, pioneering spirit, openness, strength of character, fieriness, passion, fearlessness, enthusiasm, love of adventure, combativeness, alertness, romance.

- **Weaknesses**: selfishness, aggressiveness, recklessness, carelessness, impatience, domineering, dictatorship, lack of tact, mendacity and cheating, tends to sabotage, excessiveness, intolerance, arrogance, vindictiveness, stubbornness.

### Aries Ascendant

Those with Aries on the Ascendant like change and make good use of physical exercise to dissipate their excess of mental energy, as they tend to think a lot and be impatient! While ambitious and sociable, they may experience difficulties in their relationships; and they are not the type to take advice or be swayed very easily. Practical by nature, they like to develop strategies and, being free spirits, do not care much for routine tasks. They are often talented in the use of machinery, construction, design, and scientific work. The Aries usually has few children, enjoys travelling, and may tend to oscillate between extremes.

## ♉ Taurus

- **Physical features**: medium height, muscular body, smooth face, thick neck, broad shoulders, attractive.

- **Significations**: the permanence of things, the accumulation of wealth, the pursuit of pleasure, the arts, working the land, and livestock.
- **Strengths**: productivity, business acumen, stamina, tenacity, patience, determination, stability, affection, sensuality, loyalty and fidelity, artistic sense, charismatic personality, love of good food, charm.
- **Weaknesses**: stubbornness, greed, selfishness, boredom, bigotry, possessiveness, intolerance, inflexibility, jealousy, laziness, ultraconservatism, greed, rudeness.

### Taurus Ascendant

Taurus likes to be shown affection. They have a lovely temperament and are artistic, sensual, romantic, and easily seduced by the opposite sex. They are stubborn and determined, but may become violent when angry. Rather materialistic, they can sometimes be surrounded by undesirables, but when they give their friendship, it is forever. With their sharp intellect and their physical and mental strength, they learn easily and can produce quality work. Generous and generally lucky, they do not, however, like to be supervised too closely. Taurus can be a little hard on their parents, have more girls than boys, and show the spirit of sacrifice.

## ♊ Gemini

- **Physical features**: rather tall and slim, with an erect posture and long limbs;

looks great, has fine and mobile features, a sensitive nervous system, digestive problems, and may be subject to strong sexual desire.

- **Significations**: communication, commerce, advertising, brothers and sisters, neighbours, mental energy.

- **Strengths**: ingenuity, quick wit, subtle intelligence, flexibility and adaptability, varied tastes, manual dexterity, scientific interests, keen on studies and debates, oratorical and literary talent, sociability, good judgment.

- **Weaknesses**: indecision, excessive zeal, dispersion, nervousness, irritability, mendacity and deceit, hypocrisy, irresponsibility, capriciousness, indiscretion, fickleness.

### Gemini Ascendant

Generally modest and careful in their speech, Gemini are nervous and need change, even if they sometimes have trouble making decisions. Since they are sociable by nature, they work well with others. They are talkative, jovial, quick-witted, and like playing games as well as singing, dancing, and partying. Gifted for diplomacy, trade, and all forms of communication, they easily perceive the intentions of others, but can also be quite easily fooled. They prefer an intellectually stimulating environment, enjoy travelling, and do not care much for strenuous physical tasks.

- **Physical features**: rather stout, medium height, of excellent constitution, dignified appearance, light skin, smooth features.

- **Significations**: the mother and motherhood, family, home, traditions, ancestors, education, children, privacy, emotions.

- **Strengths**: love of family and home, imagination, protective impulse, intuition, sensitivity, kindness, openness of heart, loyalty, listening, desire to have or take care of children.

- **Weaknesses**: addiction, illusion, hypersensitivity, lack of emotional autonomy, irritability, feelings of abandonment, dysfunctional relationships, greed.

### CANCER ASCENDANT

Emotional by nature and of friendly disposition and pleasant words, Cancers genuinely care for others. As changeable as the Moon, it might be difficult to understand their mood. They are intelligent and expressive, and love contact with the public. Very psychically receptive, they are also curious, romantic, shy, imaginative, and even poetic. To feel alive, they need affection, appreciation, warmth, comfort, and reassurance, and can easily be disappointed in their marital relations. Cancers are thrifty, and their vagabond nature pushes them to travel to foreign lands.

## ♌ Leo

- **Physical features**: strong physique, medium height, excellent constitution, dignified bearing, vitality, beautiful hair, and strong sexual desires.
- **Significations**: games and amusements, arts and entertainment, decorum, government, leaders, status and honours, gambling, and financial speculation.
- **Strengths**: leadership, authority, organizational aptitude, pride, ambition and vision of greatness, generosity, magnanimity, romanticism, ability to delegate, idealism, openness, confidence, aesthetic and artistic sense.
- **Weaknesses**: vanity, arrogance, haughtiness, laziness, condescension, stubborness, hunger for power, tendency to intimidate, indifference, boastfulness.

### Leo Ascendant

The Leo's life force vibrates in harmony with the Sun, which gives him a regal bearing. He wants to accomplish great things, but it may be difficult to realize his vision, and not for lack of daring! Honourable and respectful, he is self-sufficient and independent. Though sincere and sensitive, his anger can still be terrible and difficult to soothe. Despite being unpredictable, we can trust him, for he has a warm heart, and is a generous and loyal friend. He prefers positions of authority and does not like to be subordinate to an employer or boss—pride demanding. Brave and fearless, he might become a valiant and heroic member of the forces. Having a strong sex drive, he could have multiple partners.

## ♍ Virgo

- **Physical features**: medium height, thin and slender build, oval face, pleasant appearance, bright-eyed, thin voice, sensitive nervous system, slow gait.

- **Significations**: purity, method, sense of service and duty, crops, work and effort, disease, aggravations.

- **Strengths**: analytical ability, sensitivity, reserve, business instinct, insight, practicality, ingenuity, studious disposition, application, perfectionism, reliability, logic, conscientiousness, desire for purification.

- **Weaknesses**: emotional coldness, shyness, tendancy to be picky and critical, anxiety, boredom, isolation and seclusion, skepticism, servility, hypochondria, frustration, depressiveness, lack of confidence.

Virgos are constantly in search of purity, be it only physical. They are precise and methodical, yet easily bored if forced to follow a routine. They are intelligent and critical thinkers, good in mathematics and analysis, and may very well succeed in business even while keeping an active interest in many other fields of knowledge. Virgos are both impulsive—even nervous—and emotional. They enjoy art in its many forms and are willing to devote themselves to it, whether it be sculpture, design, drawing, music, or any other form of expression where great attention to detail is required. Amiable and innocent, sometimes even naive, they like conversation and are naturally curious. They usually have few children.

## ♎ LIBRA

- **Physical features**: tall or medium height, round and pleasant face, straight nose, fair complexion, graceful and attractive appearance, strong sexual desires.
- **Significations**: harmony, balance, art, justice, marriage, friendship, associations and partnerships, the couple, competition.
- **Strengths**: ability to reassure and comfort, adaptability, optimism, diplomacy, tact, grace, love, artistic sense.
- **Weaknesses**: tendency to be too accommodating, irresponsibility, ingratitude, propensity for manipulation, capriciousness, narcissism, ambivalence.

### Libra Ascendant

Libras are idealistic, with a smiling face and charitable heart. They love juggling philosophical ideas, though they tend to be mentally disorganized and emotionally unstable. Active and intelligent, they make good judges or arbitrators. They like being in the spotlight and speak frankly; they prefer to follow their own counsel and tend to hold strong opinions. Libras look for beauty and love, especially in their intimate relationships. They have a strong interest in politics and want to leave a legacy to humanity. In love with comfort, amusements, and entertainments of all kinds, they also enjoy travel and family life.

## ♏ Scorpio

- **Physical features**: medium height, robust constitution, thin, muscular, and well proportioned; curly hair, wide eyes.
- **Significations**: mysteries, life and death, the esoteric, challenges, destruction and regeneration, dangers, passions, and research.
- **Strengths**: devotion, energy, capacity for hard work, toughness, penetrating judgment, keen intelligence, supportive of relatives, deep feelings, shrewdness, generosity, intuition, instinct, strong spiritual foundation, gift of healing, ability to inspire others.
- **Weaknesses**: jealousy, selfishness, tendency to criticize and slander, possessiveness, hypersensitivity, restless

temperament, cunningness, harshness, hatred, perversion, destructive impulses, violent feelings.

### Scorpio Ascendant

Scorpios have a strong character and look for a life of excitement, preferring to avoid beaten paths. They have a reputation for being cruel and vengeful, and sometimes deserve it, but are nonetheless just as likely to be caring, sensitive, and generous. Prone to sarcasm and impulsiveness, they like to delve into mysteries and to solve enigmas, which makes them good researchers. Their erratic behaviour and a desire for instant gratification—which may lead to addictions—might adversely affect their health. Independent, secretive, and competitive, Scorpios are very determined and can become violent when angry. Interested in the creative arts, they are also skilled in the art of conversation and correspondence, and can make good teachers. Being both intelligent and capable of deep concentration, they can develop spiritual aspirations.

## ♐ Sagittarius

- **Physical features**: tall or average height, well-developed and well-proportioned body, tendency to corpulence, high forehead, graceful appearance, broad smile.
- **Significations**: the great outdoors, sport, social gatherings, dancing, long journeys abroad, religion and spirituality, law, philosophy, luck, ideals, leaders.

- **Strengths**: idealism, candour, a ready smile, strength, generosity, optimism, wisdom, independence, enthusiasm, sense of justice, high expectations, humanitarianism, philosophical mind, confidence.

- **Weaknesses**: opportunism, intolerance, religious fanaticism, greed, rudeness, rejection of authority, need for frequent change, arrogance, disobedience, rebelliousness, complacency.

### Sagittarius Ascendant

Targeting the infinity of the heavens with his bow, the Sagittarius cultivates high ideals through his daily actions. Direct, honest, and noble, he nonetheless remains humble. He hates hypocrisy, is naturally good, and loves rituals, the laws, and sacred writings. Able to exercise power without being corrupted, the Sagittarius is a good leader and he gladly sacrifices himself for the good of others. Undeterred by hard work, he will fight for a good cause, but his tendency to work long hours can lead to nervous exhaustion. A good parent and teacher, he is happy, smiling, enthusiastic, and conventional, though enterprising. He loves to travel and can find success away from his birthplace. He is also subject to domestic disputes.

## ♑ Capricorn

- **Physical features**: tall, strong upper body, but weak and thin in the lower, deep eyes, long nose.

- **Significations**: power, the state, summits, duty, loyalty, experience, ambition, responsibility, adults and elderly people, profession, setbacks, and delays.

- **Strengths**: practical sense, method, perseverance, integrity, loyalty, prudence, ingenuity, simplicity, accountability, thrift, honesty, leadership, discipline, reserve, desire to learn, capacity for hard work, need for security, love of seclusion, taste for antiquities.

- **Weaknesses**: mistrust, selfishness, rigidity, harshness, depression, anxiety, loneliness, sadness, greed, opportunism, pessimism, shyness, withdrawal, detachment, parenting out of duty rather than love.

### Capricorn Ascendant

Ambitious, persevering, and practical, the Capricorn can work for many years towards his goals. He is normally open and enthusiastic, but can also sink into melancholy and feel that he is not appreciated at his true value. Philosophical and a good organizer, he sympathizes with those less fortunate than himself. The Capricorn loves change and travel, and can adapt as needed. He has a talent for business, but is often without regard for the sensitivities of others; he can be cold, calculating, and even a little two-faced. He can achieve an enviable material status, or even high levels of spiritual or occult attainment if given the opportunity to acquire such knowledge.

- **Physical features**: medium height, sturdy build, lean, muscular, and elegant.
- **Significations**: liberty, fraternity, psychology, inventions, new technologies, the Internet and computing, progress, the unforeseen.
- **Strengths**: scientific mind, friendliness, generosity, altruism, independence, philanthropy, solitude, resourcefulness, inventiveness, empathy, nonconformity, ability to accommodate, intuition, curiosity about human behaviour, philosophical nature, keen intelligence, stoicism.
- **Weaknesses**: restlessness, stress, inflexibility, inability to follow a routine, stubbornness, eccentricity, inconstancy, rebelliousness, rudeness, lack of self-esteem, coldness, overintellectualization, isolation, depression, paranoia.

### AQUARIUS ASCENDANT

Aquarians are people who can learn a lot from their difficulties and sufferings. They may attempt to understand the laws of nature and the meaning of life, or on the other hand be purely materialistic and gloomy. The Aquarius likes to juggle with ideas and can be a writer or teacher. He is friendly and happy to help others, and his kindness makes him a very popular person. He likes social life, entertainment, sport, and studies, and often appears very intelligent. Being creative, he can work hard and may develop scientific expertise. On the other hand, he may also secretly foster bad habits. Aquarians are also subject to headaches.

## ♓ Pisces

- **Physical features**: medium or small height, rather plump body, full face, dreamy look.

- **Significations**: infinity, internalization, addiction, mysteries, mysticism, isolation, silence, hospitals, prisons, renunciation, inner life, escapism.

- **Strengths**: intuition, ability to inspire others, modesty, kindness, politeness, philosophy, vision, boundless generosity, charismatic gifts, insight, spiritual disposition, empathy, sensitivity, imagination, devotion, contemplation, benevolence, sensuality.

- **Weaknesses**: procrastination, scattering, confusion, emotionalism, sentimentality, lack of confidence, naivety, utopianism, fanciful mind, weakness, indolence, conflicting goals, anxiety, instability, fearful attitude, depression, alcoholism and other addictions.

Pisces need to help humanity, otherwise they feel miserable and adrift. They are generally good teachers. Although stubborn and changing, they remain friendly and romantic. If they feel that they are getting pushed around by life, they may seek solace in philosophy... or intoxicants. Though very intuitive, they may lack common sense and be something of a spendthrift—which does not stop them from making good bankers. Appreciated by the opposite sex, their independent and active as well as creative and imaginative nature can make them actors as well as great travellers. They are sometimes indecisive and lacking in self-confidence, but maturity benefits them greatly and brings them fortune and satisfaction.

## What Are My Signs?

Since thousands of years, the Vedic sages already knew that you would be born! And so they formulated a myriad of techniques that we, humble astrologers of today, can use to trace the outlines of your life according to the stars.

The first of these techniques—which can already provide you with a wealth of information—is to find out in which sign of the zodiac the nine planets were at the time of your birth.

Using all the data related to the planets and signs given above, here is an example of the scientific process the sages utilized to determine the influence of planets in the signs. We will here follow this method, and experiment by placing a planet in a sign, bearing the following in mind:

- Each planet has its own significations;
- Each sign is an environment in which the planets act; and
- The ruler of each sign determines the parameters within which the planets found there manifest their significations.

For the sake of example, let us say that the Sun is in Taurus.

The Sun signifies "I am", ambition, authority, confidence, dignity, influence, leadership, status and glory, vitality, power, strength, and will.

Taurus is a fixed earth sign signifying pragmatism, love of pleasure and luxury, determination, stubbornness, great vigour and stamina, productivity, need for security, lack of flexibility, artistic sense, reliability, stability, and materialism.

This combination will express itself with the oversight of Venus, which rules Taurus. Venus is the significator of acquisitions, the search for stability, concentration on owning property, an unrestrained appetite for pleasure, wealth, beauty, art, happiness, knowledge, love, comfort, luxury, harmony, and prosperity.

Result: The person who has this combination in his natal chart is someone who will seek to accumulate wealth and property, and would probably like to work in a business that focuses on beautiful things, jewellery, or luxury items such as cosmetics. He might also be a collector of fine art or a refined interior designer. Such a person will be reliable, ambitious, sensual, and determined, but simultaneously likely to be obstinate and focused on himself and his goals.

This is just a short example to illustrate some of the interactions that need to be looked at. But rest assured that the sages discussed this combination far more extensively—as they did for many other such combinations—so you can learn everything you need to know from your chart.

Now let's take a look at some examples!

Let us first take another glance at Jim Morrison's chart, this time focusing on Venus in Libra, which is its own sign, where it is all alone and living only for itself. Physically very attractive, Jim was also able to express himself artistically through his lyrics as a singer for the rock band, The Doors, as well as through his collections of poetry. His refinement reflected his sensitivity and made him look askance at the darker side of human nature. Jim was actually a scholar fascinated by learning in its broadest sense, especially where it related to social dealings, mass psychology and its manipulation, all of which is very Libra. He had countless intimate—if not purely sexual—relationships, true to the passionate, amorous, romantic, and insatiable character of Venus. The Moon's benefic aspect here also reinforced Venus' power of expression.

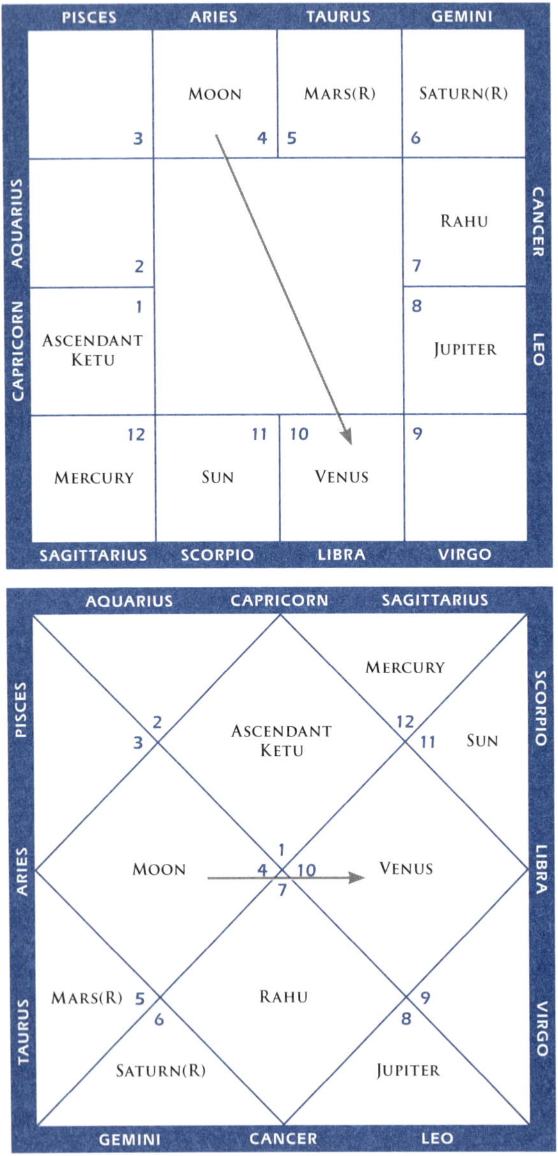


The influence of the planets — Jim Morrison

## The Influence of the Planets in the Signs

### ☉ Sun

IN ARIES ♈

*Positive side*: active, leader, courageous, generous, ambitious, warrior spirit, strong constitution, enlightened thinker.
*Negative side*: irritable, hurried, bossy, impatient, bad loser, argumentative, excited, impulsive.

IN TAURUS ♉

*Positive side*: artistic, sensual, pragmatic, conservative, determined, sophisticated, ambitious, reliable.
*Negative side*: suspicious, stubborn, obstinate, old-fashioned, self-centered, demanding.

IN GEMINI ♊

*Positive side*: bright and studious, charming, outgoing, discriminating, happy, versatile, conservative, scientific mind.
*Negative side*: unreliable, lacking originality, timid, calculating, nervous, difficult, irritable, sullen.

IN CANCER ♋

*Positive side*: sensitive, thrifty, adventurous, intuitive, sincere, persistent, dedicated, imaginative.
*Negative side*: moody, annoying, fickle, timid, dominated, hypersensitive, oversleeper, fat.

IN LEO ♌

*Positive side*: leader, ambitious, famous, brave, intelligent, independent, honest, strong vital force.

*Negative side*: authoritarian, selfish, impatient, stubborn, domineering, vain, self-centered, dogmatic.

### IN VIRGO ♍

*Positive side*: gentle, intellectual, pure in heart, analytical, healer, knows how to discriminate, sociable, intelligent.
*Negative side*: depressive, angry, critical, calculating, sentimental, naive, hypersensitive, manic about details.

### IN LIBRA ♎

*Positive side*: charming, attractive, calm, sociable, artistic, intuitive, non-violent, refined.
*Negative side*: irresponsible, lustful, inefficient, pompous, rebellious, unstable, weak.

### IN SCORPIO ♏

*Positive side*: mysterious, competitive, passionate, leader, energetic, intuitive, affectionate, attentive.
*Negative side*: controlling, aggressive, bellicose, obsessed, jealous, curt, cruel, vindictive, reckless.

### IN SAGITTARIUS ♐

*Positive side*: fair, friendly, happy, smiling, honest, optimistic, straightforward, independent.
*Negative side*: frustrated, obstinate, spoiled, idealistic, nervous, impatient, stubborn, procrastinating.

### IN CAPRICORN ♑

*Positive side*: conscientious, quiet, pragmatic, frugal, ambitious, responsible, conventional, accommodating.

*Negative side*: feels limited, workaholic, stubborn, self-centered, sceptical, depressed, isolated, humourless.

IN AQUARIUS ♒

*Positive side*: humanitarian, creative, intelligent, analytical, resourceful, friendly, dedicated, reserved.
*Negative side*: secretive, rebellious, depressed, cynical, lonely, paranoid, lacking self-esteem, victim.

IN PISCES ♓

*Positive side*: friendly, quiet, charming, idealistic, sociable, inspiring, creative, flexible.
*Negative side*: overly submissive, unreliable, victim, irritable, shy, undecided, withdrawn, sullen.

## ☽ Moon

IN ARIES ♈

*Positive side*: agile, confident, flexible, popular, healthy, talkative, bold, creative, inspiring.
*Negative side*: troubled, gullible, selfish, ambitious, deceitful, impulsive, impatient, aggressive, intolerant.

IN TAURUS ♉

*Positive side*: affectionate, popular, peaceful, generous, stable, creative, patient, pragmatic.
*Negative side*: lazy, lustful, stubborn, possessive, jealous, bland, hypersensitive, overweight.

IN GEMINI ♊

*Positive side*: sharp and creative, witty, sociable, charming, sense of humour, persuasive, scientific, intellectual.
*Negative side*: cunning, sceptical, vain, unreliable, uncertain, philandering, restless, unstable.

IN CANCER ♋

*Positive side*: imaginative, perceptive, affectionate, humane, forgiving, friendly, artistic, wise.
*Negative side*: overly impressionable, hypersensitive, anxious, servile, selfish, greedy, uncontrolled, victim.

IN LEO ♌

*Positive side*: generous, ambitious, inspiring, helpful, responsible, trustworthy, determined, straightforward.
*Negative side*: arrogant, intolerant, selfish, rowdy, proud, irritable, agitated, authoritarian.

IN VIRGO ♍

*Positive side*: refined, honest, discriminating, modest, intuitive, generous, intellectual, quick-witted.
*Negative side*: nervous, depressive, critical, compulsive, victim, hard to please, unpredictable, calculating.

IN LIBRA ♎

*Positive side*: diplomatic, persuasive, charming, gentle, gracious, refined, artistic, playful.
*Negative side*: undecided, chameleon-like, manipulative, devious, changeable, secretive, lustful.

IN SCORPIO ♏

*Positive side*: intelligent, independent, courageous, reformer, strong, open-minded, talented, intuitive.
*Negative side*: critical, lonely, indecisive, hypocritical, aggressive, heartless, severe, possessive, vengeful.

IN SAGITTARIUS ♐

*Positive side*: direct, honest, energetic, noble, determined, positive, courteous, hard-working.
*Negative side*: argumentative, aggressive, hypersensitive, sensual, rebellious, unreliable, agitated.

IN CAPRICORN ♑

*Positive side*: patient, pragmatic, thoughtful, creative, confident, ambitious, humble, reliable.
*Negative side*: heartless, unscrupulous, selfish, dogmatic, lonely, depressive, headstrong, uncertain.

IN AQUARIUS ♒

*Positive side*: creative, inventive, intuitive, visionary, mystic, philosopher, grateful.
*Negative side*: depressive, shy, weird, lonely, paranoid, nervous, critical.

IN PISCES ♓

*Positive side*: intuitive, spiritual, humanitarian, dedicated, unpretentious, respectable, loving, idealistic.
*Negative side*: servile, lazy, whimsical, naive, impulsive, irresponsible, daydreamer, hypersensitive.

## ☿ Mercury

IN ARIES ♈

*Positive side*: intelligent, resourceful, flexible, artistic.
*Negative side*: frustrated, deceptive, gambler.

IN TAURUS ♉

*Positive side*: liberal, courteous, artistic, persistent, happy.
*Negative side*: dogmatic, headstrong, frivolous.

IN GEMINI ♊

*Positive side*: good communicator, friendly, active, intelligent, inventive.
*Negative side*: superficial, hairsplitter, agitated.

IN CANCER ♋

*Positive side*: funny, sensitive, intelligent, tactful, artistic.
*Negative side*: nervous, fickle, impatient.

IN LEO ♌

*Positive side*: self-reliant, ambitious, confident, brilliant mind, inspiring.
*Negative side*: proud, stupid, misleading.

IN VIRGO ♍

*Positive side*: smart, clean, resourceful, analytical, scientific, good communicator.
*Negative side*: critical, demanding, argumentative, isolated.

IN LIBRA ♎

*Positive side*: friendly, philosophical, creative, persuasive, humanistic.
*Negative side*: lustful, irresponsible, unstable.

IN SCORPIO ♏

*Positive side*: bold, discriminating, strategic thinker, researcher, brilliant mind.
*Negative side*: selfish, impatient, paranoid.

IN SAGITTARIUS ♐

*Positive side*: wise, organized, fair, respectable, original.
*Negative side*: hasty, rash, excessive.

IN CAPRICORN ♑

*Positive side*: logical, frugal, analytical, conventional, monastic.
*Negative side*: disturbed, morose, nasty.

IN AQUARIUS ♒

*Positive side*: thoughtful, intellectual, straightforward, logical, philosophical.
*Negative side*: critical, anxious, lacking vision.

IN PISCES ♓

*Positive side*: imaginative, kind, sensitive, intuitive, analytical.
*Negative side*: absentminded, indecisive, depressed.

## ♀ VENUS

IN ARIES ♈

*Positive side*: romantic, persuasive, pleasant, playful, adventurous, generous.
*Negative side*: impatient, manipulative, goes to extremes.

### IN TAURUS ♉

*Positive side*: attractive, artistic, conciliatory, elegant, generous, respected, pleasant.
*Negative side*: lustful, lethargic, static, dependent.

### IN GEMINI ♊

*Positive side*: artistic, friendly, charming, intelligent, respected, popular.
*Negative side*: lustful, frivolous, flirtatious, naive.

### IN CANCER ♋

*Positive side*: soft, artistic, thoughtful, elegant, considerate, cultured.
*Negative side*: lustful, timid, fickle, weak.

### IN LEO ♌

*Positive side*: artistic, refined, authentic, compelling, seductive, pragmatic.
*Negative side*: proud, self-obsessed, selfish, lustful.

### IN VIRGO ♍

*Positive side*: helpful, modest, gentle, spiritual, comforting.
*Negative side*: victim, weak, servile.

### IN LIBRA ♎

*Positive side*: artistic, sensual, intuitive, passionate, enthusiastic, elegant.
*Negative side*: lustful, excessive, inconsistent.

### IN SCORPIO ♏

*Positive side*: artistic, intuitive, pleasant, active, adventurous, young at heart.
*Negative side*: jealous, vindictive, rude.

### IN SAGITTARIUS ♐

*Positive side*: respectable, influential, artistic, sensual, loyal, romantic.
*Negative side*: lustful, flamboyant, superficial, trivial.

### IN CAPRICORN ♑

*Positive side*: attractive, popular, polite, loyal, responsible, monastic.
*Negative side*: frustrated, insensitive, cold.

### IN AQUARIUS ♒

*Positive side*: amiable, friendly, sociable, independent, conventional, faithful.
*Negative side*: unrealistic, sloppy, eccentric.

### IN PISCES ♓

*Positive side*: loving, charming, polite, diplomatic, humorous, artistic.
*Negative side*: dependent, lusty, meek.

## ♂ MARS

### IN ARIES ♈

*Positive side*: energetic, competitive, pioneering, fond of sports, generous, sociable.
*Negative side*: excessively combative, ruthlessly ambitious, unreliable, extravagant.

### IN TAURUS ♉

*Positive side*: charming, seductive, sensitive, smooth talker, persuasive, considerate.
*Negative side*: intemperate, wasteful, unreliable, holier-than-thou.

IN GEMINI ♊

*Positive side*: intelligent, resourceful, attractive, clever, analytical.
*Negative side*: antisocial, cynical, restless, impatient.

IN CANCER ♋

*Positive side*: fast-thinking, independent, intelligent, grateful.
*Negative side*: irritable, disobedient, unreliable, changeable.

IN LEO ♌

*Positive side*: bold, ambitious, noble, philanthropic, liberal, competitive.
*Negative side*: angry, impatient, selfish, foolhardy.

IN VIRGO ♍

*Positive side*: independent, clever, analytical, intelligent.
*Negative side*: pretentious, deceitful, impatient, callous.

IN LIBRA ♎

*Positive side*: attractive, passionate, gentle, friendly, energetic.
*Negative side*: changing, arrogant, impatient, misleading.

IN SCORPIO ♏

*Positive side*: bright, determined, energetic, positive, passionate.
*Negative side*: vengeful, critical, stubborn, selfish.

IN SAGITTARIUS ♐

*Positive side*: direct, leader, tactician, respected, rich.

*Negative side*: self-important, impatient, manipulative.

IN CAPRICORN ♑

*Positive side*: courageous, generous, hard-working, respectable, energetic.
*Negative side*: impatient, deceptive, arrogant, obstinate.

IN AQUARIUS ♒

*Positive side*: competitive, friendly, sincere, energetic, scientific.
*Negative side*: reckless, dictatorial, frustrated, complainer.

IN PISCES ♓

*Positive side*: brave, positive, generous, friendly, affectionate.
*Negative side*: extravagant, frustrated, substance abuser, possessive.

## ♃ JUPITER

IN ARIES ♈

*Positive side*: active, friendly, patient, generous, progressive, authentic, dignified, energetic.
*Negative side*: escapist, in debt, puritanical, bold, callous, corpulent.

IN TAURUS ♉

*Positive side*: artistic, elegant, diplomatic, loved, humanitarian, tolerant.
*Negative side*: lustful, lazy, intemperate, obese, stargazer.

IN GEMINI ♊

*Positive side*: good communicator, witty, wise, writer, teacher, scholar, elegant.
*Negative side*: indifferent, escapist, several marriages, critical, neglectful.

IN CANCER ♋

*Positive side*: gentle, strong, dedicated, humane, fortunate.
*Negative side*: lustful, lazy, wishy-washy, hypersensitive.

IN LEO ♌

*Positive side*: kind, trustworthy, happy, idealistic, ethical, wise, influential.
*Negative side*: arrogant, selfish, hypersensitive, overweight.

IN VIRGO ♍

*Positive side*: enduring, learned, enthusiastic, friendly, intellectual, educated.
*Negative side*: miserly, stubborn, indecisive, impractical.

IN LIBRA ♎

*Positive side*: affectionate, friendly, sociable, humanistic, intuitive.
*Negative side*: lustful, neglectful, lazy.

IN SCORPIO ♏

*Positive side*: active, sensitive, persuasive, positive, dignified, competent.
*Negative side*: immoral, vindictive, zealous, egotistical.

### IN SAGITTARIUS ♐

*Positive side*: intelligent, wise, trustworthy, honest, influential.
*Negative side*: neglectful, unrealistic, lustful.

### IN CAPRICORN ♑

*Positive side*: persuasive, traditionalistic, pragmatic, well-organized, charitable.
*Negative side*: dreamy, pessimistic, lethargic.

### IN AQUARIUS ♒

*Positive side*: charitable, reformer, affectionate, diplomatic, self-sufficient, well-organized.
*Negative side*: heedless, lonely, inactive, moody.

### IN PISCES ♓

*Positive side*: sincere, gentle, clairvoyant, diplomatic, visionary, loving.
*Negative side*: daydreamer, lustful, impressionable, bland.

## ♄ SATURN

### IN ARIES ♈

*Positive side*: hard-working, focused, well-organized, responsible, persevering.
*Negative side*: talkative, jealous, critical, impatient.

### IN TAURUS ♉

*Positive side*: productive, self-controlled, reserved, thrifty, moderate.
*Negative side*: hesitant, neglectful, isolated, anxious.

IN GEMINI ♊

*Positive side*: concentrated, intellectual, conservative, analytical, patient, scientific.
*Negative side*: rough, compulsive, rigid, anxiety-ridden.

IN CANCER ♋

*Positive side*: humanistic, cautious, focused, stable, devoted.
*Negative side*: stubborn, pessimistic, agitated, selfish.

IN LEO ♌

*Positive side*: responsible, focused, humble, determined, reliable.
*Negative side*: stubborn, angry, depressed, cold.

IN VIRGO ♍

*Positive side*: studious, conservative, productive, focused, traditionalistic.
*Negative side*: calculating, dissatisfied, gloomy, quarrelsome.

IN LIBRA ♎

*Positive side*: concentrated, intelligent, stable, loyal, pragmatic.
*Negative side*: authoritarian, hard-working, fearful.

IN SCORPIO ♏

*Positive side*: intelligent, active, hard-working, focused, conventional.
*Negative side*: aggressive, depressive, deceitful.

IN SAGITTARIUS ♐

*Positive side*: charitable, optimistic, loyal, conscientious, respectful.

*Negative side*: servile, frustrated, lacking awareness.

IN CAPRICORN ♑
*Positive side*: concentrated, persevering, responsible, pragmatic, prudent.
*Negative side*: selfish, impatient, morose.

IN AQUARIUS ♒
*Positive side*: creative, generous, friendly, focused, analytical.
*Negative side*: passionless, alienated, depressed.

IN PISCES ♓
*Positive side*: responsible, gracious, sober, diplomatic, tolerant.
*Negative side*: solitary, naive, poor judgment.

## ☊ Rahu

IN ARIES ♈
*Positive side*: individualistic, courageous, ambitious, passionate, adventurous, fearless.
*Negative side*: selfish, stubborn, disagreeable.

IN TAURUS ♉
*Positive side*: artistic, ambitious, disciplined, pragmatic.
*Negative side*: materialistic, obstinate.

IN GEMINI ♊
*Positive side*: intelligent, intellectual, analytical, creative, exceptional.
*Negative side*: eccentric, shy, obsessive.

IN CANCER ♋

*Positive side*: attentive, intelligent, unconventional, helpful.
*Negative side*: confused, depressed, fearful.

IN LEO ♌

*Positive side*: creative, prosperous, helpful, self-sufficient.
*Negative side*: deceptive, confused, materialistic.

IN VIRGO ♍

*Positive side*: resourceful, clever, pragmatic, innovative.
*Negative side*: combative, confused, deceptive.

IN LIBRA ♎

*Positive side*: diplomatic, loving, moderate, sense of justice, sociable.
*Negative side*: misunderstood, selfish, weird.

IN SCORPIO ♏

*Positive side*: intuitive, focused, aggressive, ambitious.
*Negative side*: angry, vindictive, selfish.

IN SAGITTARIUS ♐

*Positive side*: philosophical, intelligent, witty, rich, unconventional.
*Negative side*: frightened, confused, evil.

IN CAPRICORN ♑

*Positive side*: responsible, resourceful, pragmatic, persistent, disciplined.
*Negative side*: ruthless, vicious, intense.

IN AQUARIUS ♒

*Positive side*: materialistic, creative, rich.
*Negative side*: aimless, lonely, naive.

IN PISCES ♓

*Positive side*: idealistic, philanthropic, generous, dependable.
*Negative side*: inattentive, confused, adrift.

## ☋ KETU

IN ARIES ♈

*Positive side*: active, clever, pioneer, fighter, spiritual.
*Negative side*: angry, reckless, hypersensitive.

IN TAURUS ♉

*Positive side*: ingenious, studious, intelligent, witty.
*Negative side*: hard to please, confused, indifferent.

IN GEMINI ♊

*Positive side*: intuitive, thoughtful, creative, quick, subtle.
*Negative side*: confused, calculating, impractical.

IN CANCER ♋

*Positive side*: clairvoyant, spiritual, compassionate, helpful, intuitive.
*Negative side*: unstable, nervous, worried.

IN LEO ♌

*Positive side*: spiritual, knowledgeable, flexible, powerful, pragmatic.
*Negative side*: unstable, deprives self.

IN VIRGO ♍

*Positive side*: innovative, creative, inspired, inspiring, intuitive.
*Negative side*: unstable, hypersensitive, unsatisfied.

IN LIBRA ♎

*Positive side*: sociable, flexible, versatile, well-balanced.
*Negative side*: confused, lonely, dissatisfied.

IN SCORPIO ♏

*Positive side*: expeditious, active, intuitive, intelligent.
*Negative side*: deceitful, angry, touchy.

IN SAGITTARIUS ♐

*Positive side*: humanitarian, curious, intellectual, philosopher, wealthy, mystical.
*Negative side*: immoral, scattered, unfortunate.

IN CAPRICORN ♑

*Positive side*: spiritual, creative, traditional, responsible.
*Negative side*: indifferent, stubborn, fearful.

IN AQUARIUS ♒

*Positive side*: idealistic, creative, spiritual, independent, helpful.
*Negative side*: thinks too much, in debt, isolated, unsuccessful.

IN PISCES ♓

*Positive side*: idealistic, spiritual, wise, inspiring, simple, intuitive.
*Negative side*: utopian, imprudent, victim.

Now we can add some more precise significations to the chart of our mystery star. In fact, from now on we should take into account the way the positives and negatives of the planets in the signs play a role in influencing the character, actions, and reactions of each person. So let's assess the positivity or negativity of such combinations from the data provided so far in order to capture some of the nuances in this horoscope.

Let us recall that each planet becomes bound to the lord of the sign in which it is placed. Accordingly, if the Sun is exalted in Aries, and Mars, the ruler of Aries, is situated in Cancer, it will reduce much of the promise inherent in the exaltation of the Sun. However, if the dispositor of Mars happens to be in its own sign or in exaltation, the status of Mars will be enhanced—and by extension so will that of the Sun.

And let's not forget to include the attributes of the signs as well as those of the planets!

## Exercise 2 – Exploring a Chart

### The Influence of the Planets in the Signs of Our Mystery Star

#### SUN IN SCORPIO ♏

Firstly, the water element makes it somewhat difficult for the Sun to express its individuality because water is emotional and receptive while the Sun is hot and active. This can be annoying at times, and give rise to negative attributes such as obsessiveness, abruptness, etc.

As we have already seen, the Sun here is in conjunction with Mercury and receives the aspects of three malefics. By the signs' aspects, it also receives the glances of Venus, the Moon, and Ketu.

Natal chart — Mystery star

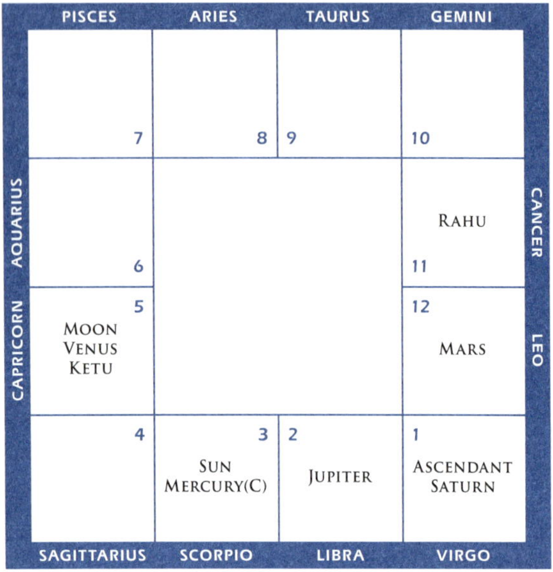


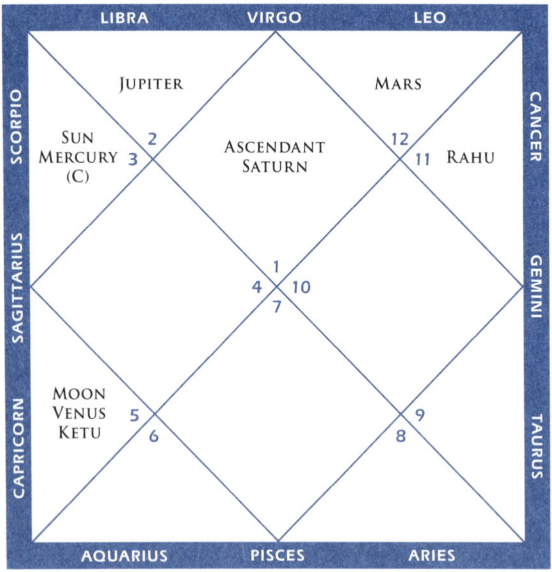

All the planets are involved here, except Jupiter. We clearly have some positive influences, but there is a lot of negative also—a great deal of negative, in fact.

The sign of Scorpio has Ketu, which is more powerful than Mars in this chart, as its dispositor. This means that it will be the object of mixed influences, since Ketu is highly benefited by its conjunction with Venus and its proximity to the Moon. There is nothing really stable about the Sun in this celestial setup, or the father figure for that matter.

*Positive side*: mysterious, competitive, passionate, leader, energetic, intuitive, affectionate, attentive.
*Negative side*: controlling, aggressive, bellicose, obsessed, jealous, curt, cruel, vindictive, reckless.

### MOON IN CAPRICORN ♑

The Moon is here afflicted by both Rahu and Ketu, while also being in conjunction with Venus. Like the Sun, the Moon receives aspects from all the malefics and benefics, except Jupiter. You will observe at first glance that Saturn does not exactly aspect the Moon, but is still closely linked to it as the ruler of Capricorn. The situation is challenging for perceptions and emotions as many influences are involved. The negative dominates—a situation bound to affect the subject's mother, also signified by the Moon. *Here's a trick: if we see in a person's life that the relative represented by an afflicted planet is also afflicted, then we know that a good part of such a planet's negativity has materialized in that way.* Anyhow, with this Moon, it is still far better to surround oneself with good company.

It is also important to observe that this Moon is the dispositor of Rahu, which is 100% unpredictable—that is, we can accurately forecast Rahu's unpredictability! We've seen that Rahu deals with issues pertaining to grandeur, compulsion, ambition, neurosis, and intoxication. Rahu's shadow will therefore taint the native's mind and will also likely reflect on her mother in different ways. In short, let's make a good note here that the dispositor of Rahu will tend to bring all kinds of surprises.

*Positive side*: patient, pragmatic, thoughtful, creative, confident, ambitious, humble, reliable.
*Negative side*: heartless, unscrupulous, selfish, dogmatic, lonely, depressed, stubborn, uncertain.

MERCURY IN SCORPIO ♏
Being in conjunction with the Sun, Mercury also receives the same influences. The intelligence may be disturbed by strange ideas or logic, and the subject may tend to rationalize her perceptions.

*Positive side*: bold, discriminating, strategic thiker, researcher, brilliant mind.
*Negative side*: selfish, impatient, paranoid.

VENUS IN CAPRICORN ♑
Venus is afflicted by Rahu and Ketu, and in conjunction with the Moon. And, like the Moon, it receives aspects from all the malefics and benefics, except Jupiter. It is located in the sign of Saturn, its friend.

The situation is not easy where relationships are concerned, as the Moon, representing the emotions, and Venus, representing love, are being used as punching bags by the malefics. Situated at the same degree as Rahu and Ketu, Venus is completely beaten down, leaving nothing but the outer shell of appearances.

*Positive side*: attractive, popular, polite, loyal, responsible, monastic.
*Negative side*: frustrated, insensitive, cold.

### MARS IN LEO ♌

Mars, the soul significator of our mystery star, is located in Leo, a friendly sign. But, as we have already seen, its neighbours are causing problems by imprisoning it. It also receives, by sign aspect, the combined influence of the Moon, Venus, Ketu, and Jupiter. With the three benefic influences, we could almost believe that its prison is golden and a source of envy for others. Will Mars find positive expression in Leo? Possibly, but only with sustained effort and most likely sporadically as we'll recall the Sun's position as Lord of Leo.

*Positive side*: bold, ambitious, noble, philanthropic, liberal, competitive.
*Negative side*: angry, impatient, selfish, imprudent.

### JUPITER IN LIBRA ♎

Jupiter is in a sociable—but not friendly—sign. Via sign aspect, it receives the influence of Mars, which stimulates passion but without deeply hurting Jupiter's significations. For example, if Mars was to aspect Jupiter by its planetary glance, it could cause physical harm to the native's child whereas this influence acts more like a Martian-tinted veil of added passion on her "wisdom". In any case, Jupiter here will act like Libra and Venus and will be concerned with love, relationships both personal and for business, the cosmetic part of things and all that awakens artful and sensual ardour. As for passion, by nature it acts on impulse rather than pragmatic considerations, hereby indicating an unbalanced approach to Libra and Venusian significations, a situation that can only lead to suffering. And since Jupiter is expansive, there will be more relationships, more artful productivity, more make-up, etc.

*Positive side*: affectionate, friendly, sociable, humanistic, intuitive.
*Negative side*: lustful, neglectful, lazy.

### SATURN IN VIRGO ♍

Saturn is in a friendly sign, and as it is only aspected by Ketu, it seems pretty relaxed. However, Saturn, which is very serious about teaching us the lessons of life, brings in its wake the Moon, Venus, and Ketu, for whom it is the dispositor, and these contribute to its productivity, albeit with ups and downs resulting from the influence of the lunar nodes.

*Positive side*: studious, conservative, productive, focused, traditionalistic.
*Negative side*: calculating, dissatisfied, gloomy, quarrelsome.

### RAHU IN CANCER ♋

Rahu, which is analytical in nature, tends to dissect emotions when in Cancer, which can cause some confusion. It is aspected by Venus, the Moon, and Ketu (always!), and through the signs' aspects, it receives the influences of the Sun and Mercury. With the help of benefics, Rahu is well placed to give rise in life.

The sign of Cancer represents the mind, perceptions, and the mother. Rahu's presence in this very sign indicates that these are problem areas, no doubt, since Rahu is related to the Moon by being in opposition to it and occupying its sign.

*Positive side*: attentive, intelligent, unconventional, helpful.
*Negative side*: confused, depressed, fearful.

### KETU IN CAPRICORN ♑

Ketu benefits from the intimate association of Venus and the Moon… that it personally irritates! This means, for example, that the subject's thinking may not be "grounded" since Ketu is a body without a head, or that her mother may not be realistic in the usual sense of the term. Ketu is influenced by all the malefics and benefics, except Jupiter. It is also associated with Saturn through its sign, which augurs a life full of surprises and lessons to learn.

*Positive side*: spiritual, creative, traditional, responsible.
*Negative side*: indifferent, stubborn, fearful.

## Tips for Exploring Your Own Chart

In our mystery celebrity's chart, we have only discussed the signs occupied by planets. Since each one of the signs indicates a great many aspects of life, it goes without saying that a concentration of benefic or malefic aspects on any of them will have an impact on its significations, even if no planet occupies it. For example, the sign of Cancer—like its lord, the Moon—represents emotions, and so it is an important area to consider when evaluating a person's emotional stability.

I hope that by practising with your own chart, you will start to discover interesting and revealing aspects of yourself. But we aren't going to stop here! Let us look next at the role the houses play in a chart.

# CHAPTER 3

# THE HOUSES

Now we turn to the astrological houses, which represent the areas in which our life experiences find expression. Each of the 12 houses represents a variety of circumstances or events, and together they cover every aspect of human existence.

## KEY SIGNIFICATIONS OF THE HOUSES

Before diving headlong into an exploration of the twelve astrological houses, let us consider some factors that will serve as a general guide to understanding the approach of the Vedic astrologers.

### THE FOUR GOALS OF LIFE

These four goals indicate the general direction of each house and the motivations of the planets in them:

- ***Dharma***: work, performance of duty, righteous action, and the application of uplifting principles of life;
- ***Artha***: economic development, wealth, business, and material progress;
- ***Kama***: sense gratification and the satisfaction of desires;

- ***Moksha***: ultimate liberation, redemption, nirvana, enlightenment, and full self-realization.

## The Elements

The four elements of fire, earth, air, and water are connected to the four goals of life and the houses as follows:

- *Dharma* houses (1, 5, and 9): fire
- *Artha* houses (2, 6, and 10): earth
- *Kama* houses (3, 7, and 11): air
- *Moksha* houses (4, 8, and 12): water

## The Spheres of Influence

- The quadrants or *kendras* (houses 1, 4, 7, and 10) are places of power and prominence where the planets are valued and where they exert concrete influence on large areas of one's life.

- The trines or *trikonas* (houses 1, 5, and 9) are the most beneficial of all the houses. They reflect one's knowledge and actual development, and give indications on how to free oneself of karma.

- The *marakas* (2 and 7) and their rulers are connected to death.

- The *upachayas* (3, 6, 10, and 11) correspond to areas where difficulties are diminished through effort, and positive results can be achieved with time. Malefic planets are very helpful there as they provide "fuel" for one's efforts.

- The *dushthanas* (6, 8, and 12) are called hidden houses because they carry notions of subconsciousness, something one cannot normally easily master. Due to this, they prove to be sources of tests and generally degrade or simply "hide" the nature of planets that occupy them.

## Benefic or Malefic?

In any astrological chart, the rulers of quadrants and trines are said to be "functional benefics," because they embody the principal orientations of human life. The functional benefics change according to the Ascendant.

When a functional benefic also happens to be the ruler of a hidden house, it retains its positive qualities, but also takes on a portion of negativity as well as a certain unpredictability, which could prove to be positive and/or negative. One then receives the individual influence of each house it rules. For example, in the case of Leo Ascendant, Jupiter is the lord of houses 5 and 8. If it is situated in the 10th house, it will produce the desirable effects of house 5—career advancement, among others—but also some adverse effects of house 8, which could result in delays, pitfalls and job changes (a stress that could prove to be for the better or not, depending on other active factors in the unfolding of destiny).

As for the rulers of houses 3, 6, and 11, they act as functional malefics, whatever the Ascendant. They represent the internal enemies (lust, anger, greed, intoxication, bewilderment, and envy), which we tend to detect more readily in others than in ourselves, and which can give one a sense of being victimized. To take the example of the Leo Ascendant, the functional malefics are Venus, Saturn, and Mercury which, as we mentioned in Chapter 1, comprise the group of lower entities.

Thus the sages decreed that some houses present more difficulties and potential for aggravation, while others favour more positive development and significant progress. Still, it's usually when things do not go as we like that we ask ourselves fundamental questions about life. Nothing happens without a reason!

## Analysis

When interpreting a chart, nothing is left to chance. Each prediction must be supported by at least three concomitant factors. We must consider each issue from every possible angle: the position of the planets, the rulers of the houses, and the dispositors of the different planets. We must also check the astrological signs, the houses occupied, and the dispositors of the houses. These are the essential bases of interpretation, to which we will soon be adding the constellations of stars. A host of interpretive techniques grow out of these foundations. It is, therefore, important to follow a methodical approach in order to discover all the determinant factors in a chart.

## The Ascendant

The first of the 12 houses in a chart is identified as the Ascendant and is of primary importance. The Ascendant and its lord actually control all the remaining positions, and their strength or weakness permeates all of life's dimensions. In other words, all other information must be considered in relation to the first house.

The ruler of the first house is always favourable, because it represents the person per se, but it might be strong or weak. Moreover, a planet in the state of fall in the first house may weaken the Ascendant as well as its lord if it is weak, situated in an unfavourable house or sign, in conjunction with a malefic planet, or badly aspected. Where appropriate, the Vedic science offers us—as we see at the end of this book—remedies for overcoming weaknesses in a chart.

Let us now look more closely at the characteristics of each house.

### House 1 • The Body

*Element*: fire
*Goal*: *dharma*
*Sphere of influence*: quadrant and trine
*Nature*: benefic
*Significator*: Sun
*Significations*: body, appearance, health, vitality, athletic ability, longevity; head, skin, and hair; birth and place of birth; infancy, early childhood, general orientation to life, and the overall strength of the horoscope; character, behaviour, virtue, honour, dignity.

### House 2 • Wealth

*Element*: earth
*Goal*: *artha*
*Sphere of influence*: *maraka*
*Nature*: malefic
*Significator*: Jupiter
*Significations*: finance, ability to earn money, accumulated wealth, clothing, jewellery, and precious metals; face and throat, vision and right eye, mouth and teeth; food and beverages, dietary habits, speech, singing, ability to converse, poetic and writing talent; family life; learning, philosophical depth, truth and lies; death.

### House 3 • Siblings

*Element*: air
*Goal*: *kama*
*Sphere of influence*: *upachaya*
*Nature*: neutral
*Significator*: Mars
*Significations*: younger siblings and our relations with them, neighbours, servants, death of parents; arms and hands, dexterity, voice, and right ear; value, vitality, strength, endurance, courage, determination, physical or mental prowess, initiative, sense of adventure; travel and moving residence; communications of all kinds, publishing, and artistic expression.

### House 4 • Family

*Element*: water
*Goal*: *moksha*
*Sphere of influence*: quadrant

*Nature*: benefic
*Significators*: Moon (also Mercury)
*Significations*: relationship with mother, kinship, inheritance, ancestors; private business, the last years of life; chest, heart, and lungs; happiness, emotions and feelings, intuition, confidence, morality, and education; residence, property, and capital; architecture, fields and farmland, vehicles and vessels; clothing, treasures, and luxuries.

### HOUSE 5 • CHILDREN

*Element*: fire
*Goal*: *dharma*
*Sphere of influence*: trine
*Nature*: benefic
*Significator*: Jupiter
*Significations*: children, sociability, emotional relationships, romance, and love received from the spouse; upper abdomen (including liver and stomach); knowledge, intelligence, insight, intuition, innocence, memory, aptitude for studying or undergoing a discipline; musical, poetic, and acting talent; taxes, business acumen, favours from highly-placed officials, politicians, advice, and advisors; sports, fun, games and speculation, the entertainment industry; piety, meditation techniques, prayer, and mantras (and the propensity for these practices); past lives.

### HOUSE 6 • ENEMIES

*Element*: earth
*Goal*: *artha*
*Sphere of influence*: *dushthana* and *upachaya*
*Nature*: malefic

*Significators*: Mars (also Saturn)
*Significations*: antagonisms and enemies, obstacles, disappointments, discouragement, competitors, and competition; theft and thieves, hate, violence, cruelty, war, and combat; maternal uncles and aunts; mid-abdomen (including the small intestine), ulcers; anxiety, irregular meals, vices, illness, pain, accidents, and injuries; employment, office, subordinate and junior positions, daily or routine work and work-related fatigue; blame, legal proceedings, and imprisonment; receipt of charitable donations; greed, credit, and debts; domestic animals, cults, distant lands, and premature death.

### House 7 • Spouse

*Element*: air
*Goal*: *kama*
*Sphere of influence*: quadrant and *maraka*
*Nature*: neutral
*Significator*: Venus
*Significations*: spouse, marriage and unions, married life, fidelity, adultery; partnerships and social interactions; lower abdomen and its organs, kidneys and urine, sexual desire, lumbar vertebrae; morals, controversy, and desire in general; the public, the world of business, associates; visible enemies and wars, foreign lands, short trips, and death.

### House 8 • Life

*Element*: water
*Goal*: *moksha*
*Sphere of influence*: *dushthana*
*Nature*: malefic

*Significator*: Saturn
*Significations*: lifespan, death; delays, setbacks, defeats; enemies, conspiracy, insults, disputes; marital problems, and cruelty; excretory system (including the colon), sexuality, and sexual organs; cancer, vitality, fatigue, psychological state, anger, chronic diseases; accidents, suffering, and fear; science, archaeology, psychology, psychoanalysis; mysticism and transcendence; inheritance and wealth obtained without work (including lotteries and insurance payments); bankruptcy, loans, taxes; poison, theft, punishment, scandal, infamy, destruction, murder, and bad news; secrets, deep and wild forests, remote places; witchcraft and black magic.

### House 9 • Knowledge

*Element*: fire
*Goal*: *dharma*
*Sphere of influence*: trine
*Nature*: benefic
*Significators*: Jupiter (also Sun)
*Significations*: luck, prosperity, wealth; beauty, knowledge, higher education, philosophy, and spirituality; relationship with father, guru, educators, counsellors, supervisors, and government; hips and thighs; publishing; politics, diplomacy, law, and justice; penance, piety, religion, good conduct, purity of spirit, worship, devotion, and pilgrimages; transport of goods and distant travels; charity and donations; grandchildren, brothers, and sisters-in-law.

### House 10 • Achievement

*Element*: earth
*Goal*: *artha*

*Sphere of influence*: quadrant and *upachaya*
*Nature*: benefic
*Significators*: Mercury (also Sun, Jupiter, Saturn)
*Significations*: vocation, profession, and career; promotions, honours, dignity, prestige, fame, success, responsibilities, power, authority; government, business, major projects, economic development, trade; personal and social status of father, kingdoms; renunciation and asceticism.

## House 11 • Earnings

*Element*: air
*Goal*: *kama*
*Sphere of influence*: *upachaya*
*Nature*: neutral
*Significator*: Jupiter
*Significations*: successes, opportunities, and possibilities; earned income, profits, liquid assets, and wealth; older brothers and sisters, paternal uncles and aunts, sons and daughters-in-law, friends, enemies of one's enemies; society, ministers, influential people, and ability to influence others; hopes, aspirations, ambitions, desires, and satisfaction of desires; ornaments, luxury, the Internet, and longevity of the mother; calves and ankles.

## House 12 • Losses

*Element*: water
*Goal*: *moksha*
*Sphere of influence*: *dushthana*
*Nature*: malefic
*Significator*: Saturn

*Significations*: expenditure and material losses; falls (physical, social, or professional); hidden enemies; separation, punishment, arrests, imprisonment; poverty, vagrancy, death, and the end of things; the quest for the Absolute, celibacy, renunciation, ashram life; illumination, salvation, the destiny of the soul after death; charity, international trade, migration; remote places, things secret, privacy; luxury items, debauchery; left foot and left eye, comfort in bed (sleep and sex), dreams; loss of limbs or vitality, hospitalization, convalescence; confusion and suicide.

Let's take another look at the chart of Adolph Hitler.

We see that his 7th house in Aries is occupied by Mars, the planet of war and conflict, which here is in its own sign. The Sun, also in Aries, occupies its sign of exaltation, which indicates a huge ego. The combination of these two malefics in a sign and a house that fortify them magnifies their power to become negative. On the other hand, they are accompanied by two benefics, Mercury and Venus, which gives the man a definite magnetism, although these two are both lords of hidden houses.

The ruler of the Ascendant is in house 7, with the 7th lord himself in house 7. As that house is simultaneously that of unions, partnerships, business associations, and social interactions, as well as of the general public, controversies, and wars, it is not surprising that the owner of this chart managed to surround himself with an army of SS and to spend so much time with his top generals developing plans to attack, invade, and "ethnically cleanse" unwanted populations.

Natal chart — Adolf Hitler

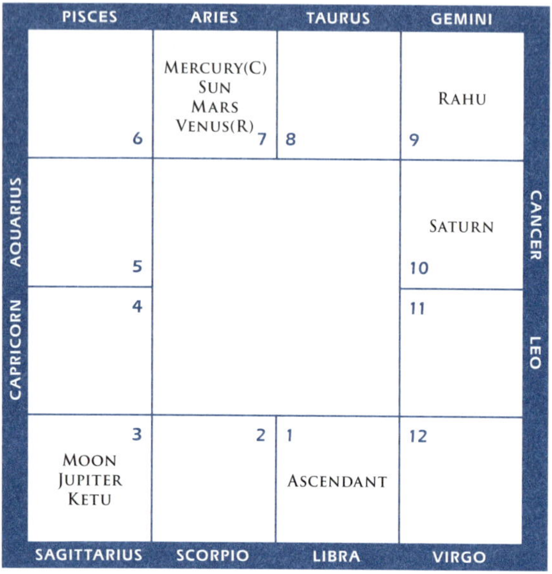


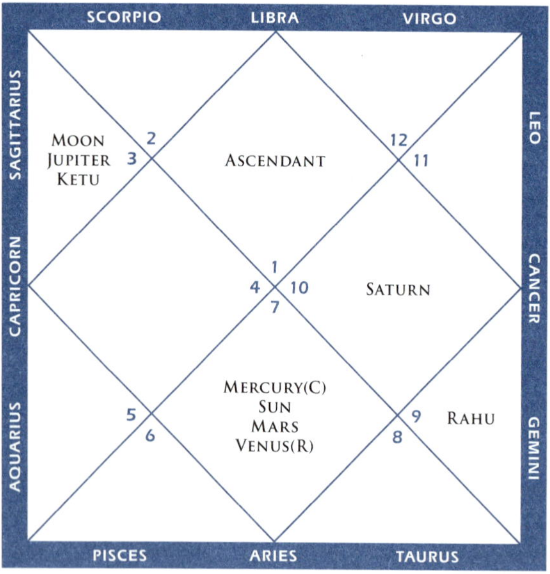

## The 9th Division of the Astrological Chart

In Vedic astrology, several systems of dividing signs are used to corroborate a chart analysis, or to examine an aspect of the native's life in greater detail. The most important of these divisional systems is called the *Navamsha*, which subdivides each sign into nine equal parts and studies the positions of the planets and the Ascendant in these sectors. Any good Vedic astrology software juxtaposes this 9th division chart to the natal horoscope.

To help us determine the strength of a planet, for example, we'll look at its location in the 9th division. Thus, if Jupiter is exalted in Cancer in the natal chart, but in fall in Capricorn in the 9th division, we will have to reduce our estimate of the positive results related to this planet.

Sometimes one or more planets occupy the same sign in both the natal and 9th division chart. This reinforces the planets in question, even if they are afflicted in the natal chart. Similarly, if the Ascendant is identical in both diagrams, it will gain much power, and its main features, regarding things such as character, health, and personality will be strengthened.

As a general rule, a weak planet in the natal chart is strengthened if it is well situated in the 9th division. Finally, this diagram allows us to evaluate the quality of a marital union by examining the 7th house and the position of Venus.

In the natal chart of Adolph Hitler, for example, we find Mars in Aries and the 7th house, a quadrant, which puts it in a position of power. In the 9th division, Mars again occupies a sign over which it rules—Scorpio—in the Ascendant, which is also a quadrant. In addition, Mars is accompanied by a benefic, which further strengthens it. The position of Mars in the 9th division therefore confirms its strength and in fact gives it more power. In the natal chart, the Moon and Jupiter occupy Sagittarius, a fire sign, whereas in the 9th division they are in Leo, another fire sign placed in the 10th house of action and career from Scorpio, which is another confirmation of the overbearing nature of this personality.

## Principles of Interpretation

It is very important to note that the Ascendant determines the location of houses where the active elements of the astrological chart, the planets, exert their influence as lords of the houses they rule. We will therefore consider the planetary positions in this light.

Moreover, it is a golden rule that one should examine the positions of all the planets from the vantage point of the Moon, which in this perspective acts as an Ascendant or 1st house.

We should also use the Sun's position as an Ascendant to find out whether other important information can be found on the horizon. An examination of a chart from this angle is particularly useful when looking at the planetary periods as they change over a person's lifetime.

When three or more indicators point in the same direction, we can conclude that a factor found in the

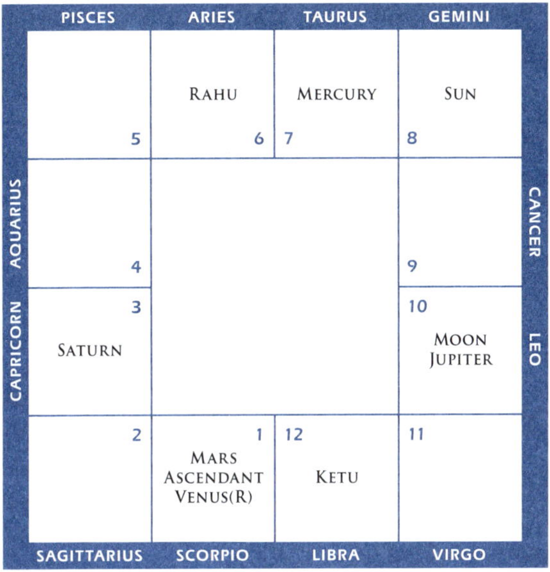


9th division — Adolf Hitler

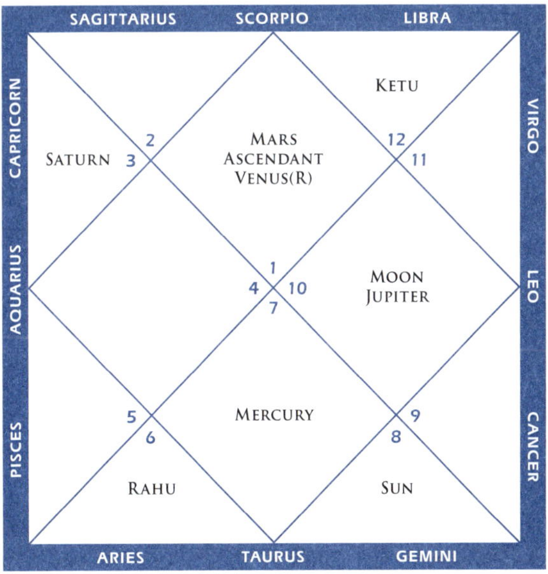

natal chart is dominant. Moreover, as we have seen, a single planet or house can simultaneously affect several aspects of our lives. It must therefore be concluded that an afflicted Sun, for example, not only disrupts our self-esteem, but perhaps also our relationships with others, the types of jobs we occupy, and the kind of money we make from them.

Let us take this opportunity to highlight another important principle: when the lord of a house is in the 6th, 8th, or 12th house from the one it rules, this will probably result in difficulties, setbacks, or losses in due time. For example, if the Moon, which governs the sign of Cancer, is in Gemini, it is in the 12th house from its sign, a position that can indicate losses related to the significations of Cancer and the house this sign is occupying. So, if Cancer is occupying the 7th house, the losses or difficulties in question may be related to the spouse.

We are now ready to take the crucial step of examining your chart from the above three perspectives in order to extract relevant information regarding:

- Personality and health;
- Career;
- Wealth;
- Personal relations; and
- Spirituality.

What follows will help you in examining the essential factors that need to be verified. The data obtained should be added to what you have already learned and will specify the areas in which the meanings of the planets and signs will be expressed.

## Personality and Health

We must here determine the quality of the Ascendant. The influence of natural malefics on the Ascendant or its ruler can indicate health problems. If three malefics are involved, things may deteriorate badly. Other clues:

- Is the lord of the Ascendant strong in the sign where it is placed? Which planet is its ruler and where is it?
- What is the relationship between the Ascendant and its ruler and the hidden houses (6, 8, and 12) and their lords?
- Check the position of the lord of the Ascendant and its dispositor in the 9th division. Are they in the same sign as in the birth chart, exalted in their own sign, or in fall?

## Career

Pay particular attention to the following factors:

- The 10th house, its ruler and its position, the aspects given and received, as well as the significations of the sign in the 10th house.
- You can also locate the position of the lord of the 10th house in the 9th division and check who is the ruler of the house it occupies, since its nature and

significations will have an influence on the career.

### Wealth

- The money houses are the 2nd, the 11th, and the trines, i.e., houses 1, 5, and 9. A positive relationship between these houses, their rulers, and the Ascendant or its lord is a guarantee of financial health.
- The favourable or unfavourable placement in the 9th division of the elements seen in the natal chart will accentuate or reduce the influences that you have identified there.

### Relationships

- *Emotions*: Look to the 4th house and its ruler, the sign of Cancer, and the Moon. Malefic influences—particularly of Rahu and Ketu—or aspects received from them can cause emotional distress and harm relations.
- *Children*: The 5th house, its lord, and Jupiter.
- *Family life*: The 2nd house and its ruler.
- *Love life*: The 5th house and its ruler.
- *Marriage and partners*: The 7th house and its lord, as well as Venus, the general significator for relationships, especially

the spouse for a male subject. (Jupiter is normally the spouse for a female subject.)

- *Sex life*: The 8th house and its ruler for sexual vitality. The 12th house and its lord for sexual pleasure.
- *Marital relationship*: Since the 9th division is representative of the marital relationship, you can also examine the 7th house there for more information on the partner, as well as the position of Venus for men, or Jupiter for women.

### Spirituality

To determine the path most conducive to spiritual development, the influences of Jupiter, Saturn, and Mercury should be checked. What you should look for is whether one or more of these are connected to the 1st house or its ruler, to the Sun, or to the Moon. If one of these three planets is lord of the Ascendant, its influence increases.

- Jupiter denotes an inner life more focused on prayer and devotion.
- Saturn indicates that self-realization will rather go through introspection, the practice of meditation, austerity, detachment from sensory pleasures, or monasticism.
- Mercury means that spiritual progress will be made preferably by the quest for truth, the study of sacred texts, Zen discipline, or the practice of astrology.

If several of these factors are combined, one's spiritual development can result from converging approaches.

By now you will have understood that you have to consider a chart from a variety of angles, and that with the integration of the astrological houses and the 9th division, things really start becoming much clearer and more precise.

Let's see what happens if we look at the most salient of these points in our mystery celebrity's chart.

## Exercise 3 – Exploring a Chart

### The Influence of the Houses on Our Mystery Star

#### PERSONALITY AND HEALTH

*Virgo Ascendant*: As we have seen in the table on page 39 ("Houses of fall"), Saturn in the perfectionist sign of Virgo is in a situation of fall in the 1st house, where it has a constricting effect on the personality. As the lord of houses 5 and 6 (Capricorn and Aquarius), however, Saturn transmits the athletic, creative, artistic, and romantic attributes of the 5th house to the Ascendant, combined with the competitive and combative attributes of the 6th, all of which are desirable influences for an accomplished dancer.

The only aspect received by the Ascendant comes from Ketu, ruler of house 3, signifying arts and communications. Ketu carries with it the influence of Venus, lord of house 2, signifying song, speech, the face, throat, and money, as well as that of house 9—luck, prosperity, splendour, good fortune—and that of the Moon, lord of house 11—desires, aspirations, the legs (as we were saying, a singer and dancer...), and money!

*Lord of the Ascendant and Sun in Scorpio*: Mercury, ruler of the Ascendant, is placed in house 3, which most notably fosters vitality, courage, communication, arts, and creativity; but it is in the secret and mysterious sign of Scorpio, a water sign where it is not comfortable. Its conjunction with the Sun indicates that the significations of house 3 are of double importance in our mystery celebrity's life, and that her intelligence is active in this sphere of activities.

The aspects of all the malefics in the chart fall on the Ascendant lord—Mercury, the planet of the intellect—as well as on the Sun and the Moon. All this portends mental health problems with possible implications for physical health over time, coupled with a marked tendency to self-destruction.

*Dispositor of the lord of the Ascendant in Capricorn*: Ketu, the dispositor of Mercury, is in house 5 along with two natural benefics. Our star will therefore develop in an environment where intelligence, creativity, business savvy, fun, love, and other meanings of this house are in evidence.

*Ascending Moon in Capricorn*: In examining the chart from the vantage point of the Moon, we find that Saturn, the dispositor of the Moon in Capricorn, occupies the 9th house in Virgo—a friendly sign and a house of good fortune—a position that might indicate a sort of religious or philosophical leader (9th house stuff) who is at the same time somewhat calculating, or even deliberately misleading (Virgo, sign of business).

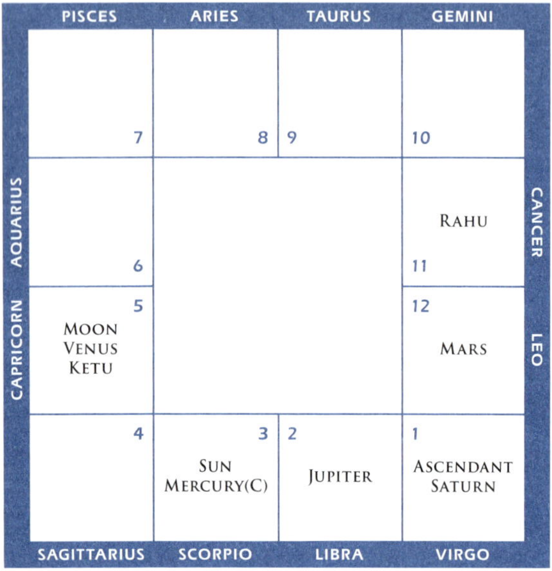


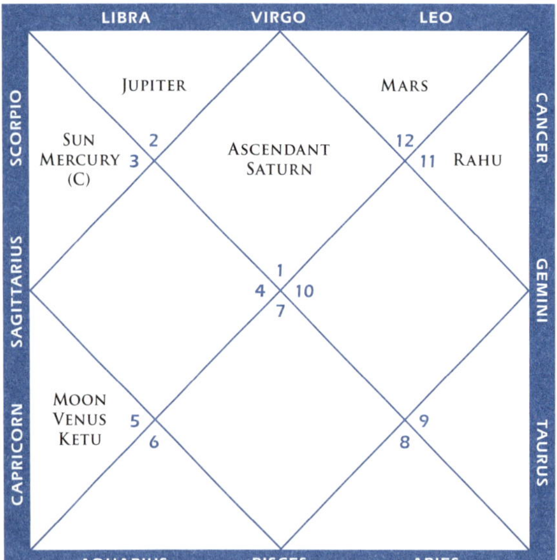


Natal chart — Mystery star

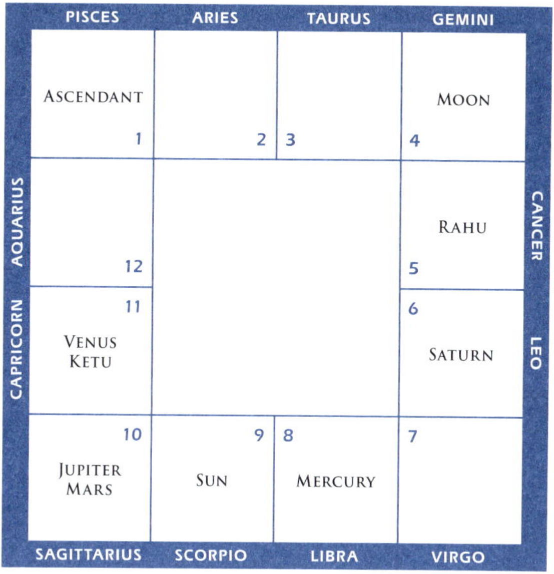
PISCES
ARIES
TAURUS
GEMINI
ASCENDANT
1
2
3
MOON
4
AQUARIUS
12
RAHU
5
CANCER
CAPRICORN
11
VENUS
KETU
6
SATURN
LEO
10
JUPITER
MARS
9
SUN
8
MERCURY
7
SAGITTARIUS
SCORPIO
LIBRA
VIRGO

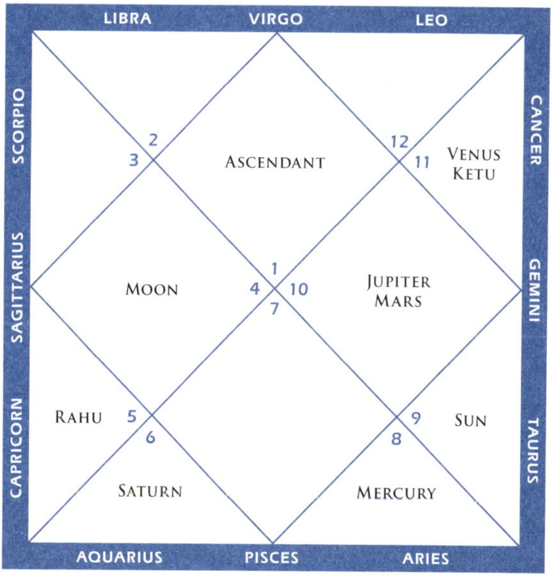
LIBRA
VIRGO
LEO
SCORPIO
2
3
ASCENDANT
12
11
VENUS
KETU
CANCER
SAGITTARIUS
MOON
1
4
10
7
JUPITER
MARS
GEMINI
CAPRICORN
RAHU
5
6
SATURN
9
SUN
8
MERCURY
TAURUS
AQUARIUS
PISCES
ARIES

For a Capricorn Ascendant, Venus simultaneously governs houses 5 and 10. So we are here dealing with a strong Venus that is transmitting its influence to the lunar nodes that dominate it, thereby producing a combination that fosters talent, sensuality, and visibility, all in the axis of houses 1 and 7, which are directly related to the public and business.

*Solar Ascendant in Scorpio*: Taking the Sun as the Ascendant, we see that the very influential combination taking place in Capricorn acts on the axis of houses 3 and 9, indicating once again that the arts and communication are part of our star's natural assets. Indeed, given the strength of the sign of Capricorn, we must conclude that the Lunar Ascendant is dominant in this chart.

*The 9th division*: Here, Mercury occupies the sociable sign of Libra in house 8, a difficult position emphasizing relationships (Libra) and sex-appeal (house 8). Its dispositor, Venus, is conjunct with Ketu in Capricorn, as in the natal chart. The repetition of this combination gives more weight to its influence, especially as it occurs in house 11, the place of desires, aspirations, and profits, areas where we would expect a Ketu influence to sprinkle some losses as time sees fit.

#### CAREER

*The 10th house and its ruler*: The fact that Mercury, the lord of the Ascendant, also governs the 10th house shows the great influence that the 3rd house of communication and the mysterious sign of Scorpio will have on our star's career—indicating secret communications or revelations.

From the Moon's position, Jupiter occupies the artistic sign of Libra in house 10 as ruler of house 3, which also connects career to the significations of this house and its lord, particularly with respect to prestige and fame. Moreover, Jupiter also governs the 12th house of remote locations, expenses... and intimate pleasures, all of which can also have an effect on the career.

Rahu occupies the 7th house, which implies business associates who have an awareness of psychology or scientifically proven methods of manipulation, in the sensitive sign of Cancer. This would imply skill in playing on people's emotions.

From the Sun, Mars—the soul significator—occupies the 10th house in Leo, the sign of the arts, entertainment, and show business, which is well known to indicate exhibitionistic tendencies. The 10th house is also an *upachaya,* a house where things improve with effort over time. The framing of house 10 by two malefics, however, means that painful ups and downs are inevitable.

*The 9th division:* The position of the ruler of house 10 (Mercury) in Libra in the 9th division once again connects Venus and all its artistic, aesthetic, and sensuous trappings to the native's career. Given its location in the 8th house, you can add to that a liberal dose of sex, along with plenty of obstacles and disappointments.

FINANCES

*From the Ascendant*: Since the 5th house is one of good fortune and Ketu is situated at the same degree as Venus, lord of houses 2 and 9, while in conjunction with the Moon, ruler of house 11, undertakings related to house 3 and the sign of Scorpio will certainly be profitable. The influence of all the planets except Jupiter on the 5th house indicates, however, that some heavy karma has accumulated at this point of the horoscope, pointing to inevitable ups and downs, that is to say, many situations where our featured star will need to make great efforts just to keep afloat, be it romance, children, discernment, or the entertainment industry. Still, the nodes of the Moon in the karmic axis of houses 5 and 11—where money "feels good"—enjoy the intimate company of Venus (our star's fortune was estimated at $US 120,000,000 in 2007—with investments earning her $US 4,000,000 per year!)

*From the position of the Moon in Capricorn*: Rahu governs the 2nd house (taking into consideration that Rahu is in direct relationship with three other planets, and therefore more powerful than Saturn) and also occupies the 7th house, a house of power, with the lords of houses 5, 7, 10, and 11—another very friendly and profitable relationship.

*From the position of the Sun in Scorpio*: Jupiter alone governs houses 2 and 5. Located in house 12, it can bring monetary gains from abroad and expenses from nowhere!

The Sun, lord of house 10, is in conjunction with Mercury, the lord of house 11, which unambiguously indicates gains from professional work.

*The 9th division*: All the elements of the natal chart are particularly well situated in the 9th division, except for Mercury in the 8th house. The result is a solid, indeed, quite enviable financial situation.

#### PERSONAL RELATIONS

*Emotions*: As observed earlier, the waxing Moon is afflicted by the lunar nodes and all the malefics in the chart. The sign of Cancer, also afflicted by the lunar nodes, however, receives aspects from the three natural benefics—the Moon, Venus, and Mercury—which helps soothe our celebrity's somewhat turbulent and at times difficult to control emotions.

The 4th house in Sagittarius receives a restrictive sign aspect from Saturn and is wedged between the Sun in Scorpio and Ketu in Capricorn, which is not really great for emotional balance. The 4th house from the Moon, in Aries, receives an aspect from the magnificent Jupiter, as it does from the Sun Ascendant, which can help our star stay within the bounds of what is socially acceptable, but without any real guarantee.

*Children, family life, love, and partners*: From the Ascendant, Jupiter occupies house 2. From the Moon, the 2nd house in Aquarius receives the aspects of Mars and Rahu, but also of Jupiter, which reduces conflicts and troubles caused by these two malefics.

From the Sun, Jupiter governs house 2 in Sagittarius. Located in house 11 from its sign of Sagittarius, it indicates gains through the family. Alas, Jupiter being in the 12th house from the Sun also shows many unwanted expenses related to 2nd house matters.

In terms of personal relationships, the Moon and Venus, our significators, are under the influence of several malefics, all of which are intimately connected to the emotions. Jupiter (considered here to be the woman's partner) governs the 7th house in Pisces, which receives aspects from Saturn, Mars, and Rahu, a guarantee of serious difficulties. Moreover, Jupiter is placed in the 8th house, a hidden house, from its sign of Pisces, which definitively suggests problems… that may not remain hidden! Although the Moon and Venus are in house 5, the lunar nodes awkwardly taint the love that is received.

From the Moon, houses 1 and 7 are afflicted in the Rahu-Ketu axis, meaning surprises and the unexpected. In addition, Venus, the ruler of house 5 in Taurus, is in difficulty due to the lunar nodes and other malefics, which again shows that surprises will abound, while love received from the spouse and the subject's relationship with her children will suffer, as will she.

Rahu in house 7 indicates that there will be a lack of support from the spouse or business partners. As the 7th house also represents the public, this could mean a reduction in our star's fan base. Problems and surprises of all kinds are repeated from different angles, which do not portend a very happy and emotionally fulfilling life.

*The 9th division*: Virgo in the 7th house of the 9th division chart presages a spouse who is both meticulous and a perfectionist, to the point of being picky and quick to criticize. Virgo also being a sign of business, the girl's hero should well be able to calculate what is beneficial for his own sake. Mercury, the lord of the 7th house occupies the 8th, a position that further indicates inevitable problems and disappointments in regard to marital life.

Libra is a sociable sign, indicating that the native's social circle might be partly responsible for the difficulties she will go through. In the 9th division, Jupiter, the spouse significator for a woman, is strong and dominant, and in conjunction with Mars, which suggests that our goddess could tie the knot with a passionate knight in shining armour, after which the inevitable conflicts arise.

#### SPIRITUALITY

Saturn in the Ascendant aspects the Sun and is moreover the dispositor of the Moon, which indicates an ability to undertake austerities, but probably not geared at transcendence, given the generally materialistic orientation of this chart.

### Tips for Exploring Your Own Chart

Which brings us to another little trick: when you find out where the lord of your Ascendant is, and then the dispositor of the Ascendant's ruler, you will find out where you spend most of your time: at the factory, office, university, church, home, or elsewhere.

In our example, we used the significations of the houses which their lords carry with them—as dispositors, each becomes a temporary benefic or malefic ruler according to the Ascendant. In addition, we have considered their natural benefic or malefic quality. So, according to its location or its aspects, each planet carries several meanings that can sometimes seem contradictory. But isn't that the way life is? For, something that might bring success and joy in one part of our life may simultaneously cause us much grief in another.

# CHAPTER 4

# THE CONSTELLATIONS

Each of the 27 divisions of the lunar zodiac corresponds to a constellation. Even though a constellation consists of more than one star, it is common usage in astrology to refer to an entire constellation by simply qualifying it as a star.

Over its cycle, the Moon passes through the 27 starry constellations at the rate of one constellation a day.

## THE VERY FIRST STAR WARS

In order to illustrate the waxing and waning phases of the Moon, Vedic mythology tells the following story.

The Moon, the male principle, married 27 sisters, all daughters of an illustrious personality whose function was to populate the newly created universe. As one might suspect, the Moon had a favourite among the 27, the one among them who was most beautiful and sweetest in character. Being naturally more attached to her, he spent most of his time with her. Seeing this as an injustice, the other 26 sisters complained to their powerful father who cursed the Moon to die on the spot.

After the death of their spouse, the 26 less sought-after sisters realized that when their husband lived, he spent at least some of the time with each of them, whereas now they were completely deprived of his company! They, therefore, returned to ask their influent father to bring the Moon back to life with his mystic powers. He admitted to them he did not have this ability, and said he could only change his curse in a way that the Moon would have to die and come back to life in repeated cycles. And so it came to pass.

## Practically Speaking

The Moon represents the mind and emotions. The story of the 27 wives means that the Moon easily and regularly changes attitudes vis-à-vis the questions or problems of life. Not only does it visit each of the 27 constellations in 27 days, but on each of its visits, it is at a different phase of its waxing and waning cycle since this cycle lasts 29.5 days, which demonstrates not only the Moon's flexibility, but its vulnerability as well.

The position of the Moon in the birth chart is one of the main indicators of one's natural way of seeing things; and the degree to which it is located in a constellation is used to calculate the most significant periods of influence of the different planets over the course of one's life.

So, the sages ascribed to each constellation a name, a ruling planet, a particular temperament, and a quality, along with other attributes. Thus the 27 constellations or stars are governed by the seven planets and the two lunar nodes, and are further divided into three groups of nine, corresponding to three segments of the zodiac, from Aries to Cancer, Leo to Scorpio, and Sagittarius to Pisces. As far as their names are concerned, since their scientific designation is no more familiar to ordinary people than the Sanskrit one, we will simply use the traditional terminology.

The constellations are counted starting from 0 degrees in Aries, each one covering 13°20′, while their lords come in the following sequence: Ketu, Venus, Sun, Moon, Mars, Rahu, Jupiter, Saturn, and Mercury. And this sequence is repeated three times. In addition, each constellation is further subdivided into four sections of 3°20′ that serve to establish the 9th division of one's birth chart. The exact figures are given in the table appearing on pages 176-179.

The constellations manifest their influence only when they are "activated" by a planet in the natal chart, or during a planetary transit, which we discuss later.

## The Constellations' Table

### Character

- **Divine**: a virtuous and benevolent disposition.

- **Demonic**: a grossly materialistic and malignant disposition.

- **Human**: a disposition alternating between virtue and materialism, according to one's moods.

### Quality

This classification is useful when it comes to choosing the best time for holding an event based on transits or the Moon's journey of the Moon through the stars. In brief, here is an overview of the qualities and the activities appropriate to them:

| Sign | Constellations (sections) | Degrees |
|---|---|---|
| Aries ♈ | Ashwini (1-4) | 0° to 13°20' |
| | Bharani (1-4) | 13°20' to 26°40' |
| | Krittika (1) | 26°40' to 30°00' |
| Taurus ♉ | Krittika (2-4) | 0° to 10°00' |
| | Rohini (1-4) | 10°00' to 23°20' |
| | Mrigashira (1, 2) | 23°20' to 30°00' |
| Gemini ♊ | Mrigashira (3, 4) | 0° to 06°40' |
| | Ardra (1-4) | 06°40' to 20°00' |
| | Punarvasu (1-3) | 20°00' to 30°00' |
| Cancer ♋ | Punarvasu (4) | 0° to 03°20' |
| | Pushya (1-4) | 03°20' to 16°40' |
| | Ashlesha (1-4) | 16°40' to 30°00' |
| Leo ♌ | Magha (1-4) | 0° to 13°20' |
| | Purva Phalguni (1-4) | 13°20' to 26°40' |
| | Uttara Phalguni (1) | 26°40' to 30°00' |
| Virgo ♍ | Uttara Phalguni (2-4) | 0° to 10°00' |
| | Hasta (1-4) | 10°00' to 23°20' |
| | Chitra (1, 2) | 23°20' to 30°00' |

| Lord | Character | Quality |
| --- | --- | --- |
| Ketu | Divine | Light/swift |
| Venus | Human | Violent |
| Sun | Demoniac | Mixed |
| Sun | Demoniac | Mixed |
| Moon | Human | Fixed |
| Mars | Divine | Soft |
| Mars | Divine | Soft |
| Rahu | Demoniac | Sharp |
| Jupiter | Divine | Movable |
| Jupiter | Divine | Movable |
| Saturn | Divine | Light/swift |
| Mercury | Demoniac | Sharp |
| Ketu | Demoniac | Violent |
| Venus | Human | Fixed |
| Sun | Human | Fixed |
| Sun | Human | Fixed |
| Moon | Divine | Light/swift |
| Mars | Demoniac | Soft |

| Sign | Constellations (sections) | Degrees |
|---|---|---|
| Libra ♎ | Chitra (3, 4) | 0° to 06°40' |
| | Swati (1-4) | 06°40' to 20°00' |
| | Vishakha (1-3) | 20°00' to 30°00' |
| Scorpio ♏ | Vishakha (4) | 0° to 03°20' |
| | Anuradha (1-4) | 03°20' to 16°40' |
| | Jyeshtha (1-4) | 16°40' to 30°00' |
| Sagittarius ♐ | Mula (1-4) | 0° to 13°20' |
| | Purvashadha (1-4) | 13°20' to 26°40' |
| | Uttarashadha (1) | 26°40' to 30°00' |
| Capricorn ♑ | Uttarashadha (2-4) | 0° to 10°00' |
| | Shravana (1-4) | 10°00' to 23°20' |
| | Dhanishtha (1, 2) | 23°20' to 30°00' |
| Aquarius ♒ | Dhanishtha (3, 4) | 0° to 06°40' |
| | Shatabhisha (1-4) | 06°40' to 20°00' |
| | Purva Bhadrapada (1-3) | 20°00' to 30°00' |
| Pisces ♓ | Purva Bhadrapada (4) | 0° to 03°20' |
| | Uttara Bhadrapada (1-4) | 03°20' to 16°40' |
| | Revati (1-4) | 16°40' to 30°00' |

| Lord | Character | Quality |
|---|---|---|
| Mars | Demoniac | Soft |
| Rahu | Divine | Movable |
| Jupiter | Demoniac | Mixed |
| Jupiter | Demoniac | Mixed |
| Saturn | Divine | Soft |
| Mercury | Demoniac | Sharp |
| Ketu | Demoniac | Sharp |
| Venus | Human | Violent |
| Sun | Human | Fixed |
| Sun | Human | Fixed |
| Moon | Divine | Movable |
| Mars | Demoniac | Movable |
| Mars | Demoniac | Movable |
| Rahu | Demoniac | Movable |
| Jupiter | Human | Violent |
| Jupiter | Human | Violent |
| Saturn | Human | Fixed |
| Mercury | Divine | Soft |

- **Light / swift**: leaving on a trip, sports activity, treating a disease or giving medication, starting a new business, concluding a sale, and repaying debts.

- **Soft**: studying music, dance, and drama, celebrating a ceremony (like marriage), buying and wearing new clothes, engaging in intimate exchanges, making new friends, and benefiting from revitalizing pleasures.

- **Fixed**: building a house, starting a community, cultivating the land, planting trees, and buying a farm property.

- **Movable**: buying a car, attending a parade or a demonstration, gardening and landscaping, changing residence or career, travelling, or initiating any activity that marks a major change.

- **Sharp**: separating from a friend or spouse, undertaking bold actions, invoking spirits, reciting incantations, practicing black magic, casting spells, exorcism, punishing, or even killing.

- **Violent**: setting fire, poisoning, destroying property, and other unhealthy acts; imprisonment or some other form of containment can be experienced here.

- **Mixed**: generally good for common social activities.

The previous table can be used to quickly determine the position of a planet in the constellations and to draw key information from it.

For example, if Jupiter is at 19° in Aries, it occupies the *Bharani* constellation, whose lord is Venus. Jupiter will not only be influenced by the sign of Aries and its lord Mars, but also by Venus. As the Mars-Venus combination emits a lot of passionate energy, Jupiter here is functioning in an environment focused on fulfilling intense desires rooted in materialism and sexuality.

Or, if the Moon occupies the constellation *Jyeshtha* in Scorpio, which is ruled by Mercury and located in a sign governed by Mars, the mind becomes sharp, incisive, lucid, realistic, and highly imaginative. The Mars-Mercury combination reflects an intellectual passion that colours the Moon and all its perceptions.

It should be mentioned here that the Moon's waxing phase is always considered the best for undertaking major projects like travel, job search, etc. This is another factor to consider if one wants to take advantage of favourable stars.

## A Description of the Constellations

### *Ashwini* • The Sun is exalted in *Ashwini*

*Symbol*: horse head.
*Personal traits*: handsome, bright, and very attractive to the opposite sex, strong, powerful, active, deeply intuitive, strives for perfection and challenges, passionate, natural healer, full of innocence and idealism, seeks virtue, and emphasizes duty (*dharma).*

This vigorous and energetic constellation gives the power to heal and to attain one's goal.

### Bharani

*Symbol*: female sex organ.
*Personal traits*: sensual, love of beauty and art, need for physical proximity, seeks harmony, attempts to meet one's needs on a purely physical level, impatient, and motivated by the satisfaction of material desires (*artha)*. This star of creative power is related to birth and death, and also has the power to cleanse and remove impurities.

### Krittika • The Moon is exalted in Krittika

*Symbol*: razor or knife.
*Personal traits*: very intelligent warrior who defends and protects, subject to anger, simultaneously outgoing and puritanical, admired because of his appearance, motivated by desire and passion (*kama)*. This star, which underlies the need to neutralize unfavourable factors, gives the power to overcome negativity to reach the truth.

### Rohini

*Symbol*: chariot (symbol of royalty).
*Personal traits*: great beauty, perfection, searches for the feminine essence, emotional, sensitive, mysterious, charming, passionate, vulnerable to addictions, jealous, romantic, seeks excellence through dedication to the beloved or to God (*moksha)*. This star signifies the conquest of hearts and promotes growth and creation.

## Mrigashira

*Symbol*: deer's head.
*Personal traits*: strongly individualistic, keen intelligence, bright mind, likes action, sports and new challenges, unstable, easily bored, impulsive and wilful, sensitive to criticism, dramatic, leader, seeks excellence through carrying out a mission (*moksha*). This thinker and researcher star gives the power to achieve one's goals.

## Ardra

*Symbol*: human head.
*Personal traits*: popular and successful, active, understands different points of view, athletic, lover of music, writing, and drama, skilled in computer sciences, friendly, ambitious, wants to better himself, self-demanding, idealistic, motivated by desire and passion (*kama*). This star represents the totality of one's karma and gives the power to succeed by one's own sustained efforts.

## Punarvasu

*Symbol*: bow.
*Personal traits*: affectionate, attentive, good guide and counsellor, ambitious, loves family and companionship, friendly, needs to be active, fond of sports, emotional and intellectual, capable of detachment, motivated by practical things (*artha*). This star, which creates a link between action and its goals, gives the power to obtain wealth and abundance.

*Symbol*: flower.
*Personal traits*: responsible, hard-working, creative, imaginative, pragmatic, loves knowledge, blind to his own qualities, good-looking, needs quiet, tolerant of pain, serene, strives for virtue in action, and emphasizes duty (*dharma*). This star, which blossoms for the pleasure of others, unconscious of its own beauty, gives the power to seize the spiritual energy.

## ASHLESHA

*Symbol*: cobra.
*Personal traits*: hypnotic eyes, acute vision of nature's secrets, wisdom, active mind, solitary, independent, creative, likes quiet and meditation, scathing humour, good advisor, attractive and uses his attractiveness to achieve his goals, seeks virtue in action, and emphasizes duty (*dharma*). This star, which symbolizes wisdom, rebirth, transformation, and the evolution of consciousness, has the power to poison.

## MAGHA

*Symbol*: palanquin.
*Personal traits*: attracts friends and admirers, clever and intelligent leader, power-hungry, politician, possesses kindness and quiet strength, traditionalistic, stubborn, non-violent, trustworthy, pleasant, loves life, sometimes arrogant, hot-tempered, motivated by anything that is down-to-earth (*artha*). This star is connected to a profound and divine spirituality, and gives one the power to travel outside the body.

## Purva Phalguni

*Symbol*: home.
*Personal traits*: lucky, charismatic, charming, warm, energetic, loves kids, good parent, goes through life without major obstacles, sincere and direct, is the center of attention, likes comfort, sensual, motivated by desire and passion (*kama*). This star of warm conviviality bestows the power of creativity and procreation.

## Uttara Phalguni

*Symbol*: bed.
*Personal traits*: generous to all, friendly, warm, charismatic, attractive, serves as an example, ambitious, hard-working, virile, strong, brave, good strategist or politician, insecure and tense, trustworthy, motivated by a proper vision of reality, beyond the material (*moksha*). This star evokes sexual energy and entanglement in matter, and gives the power to acquire wealth through marriage.

## Hasta • Mercury is exalted in Hasta

*Symbol*: hand.
*Personal traits*: charming, interesting and beautiful, seems materialistic, but is looking for more than material success, as moody as the Moon, lucky, hard-working, ambitious, responsible, motivated by the quest for the highest degree of perfection (*moksha*). This star, like a reservoir holding the entire fate of an individual, has the power to manifest the very thing one is looking for.

## Chitra

*Symbol*: pearl.
*Personal traits*: attractive, charismatic, intelligent, natural leader, sociable but solitary by nature, athletic, likes unusual clothing, creative, pragmatic, intuitive, unstable, easily bored, theatrical, loves life on a grand scale, courageous, has a strong personality, is motivated by passion and the desire to experience life fully *(kama)*. This star, like a pearl which has developed in the shell over many years, gives one the power to accumulate merit in this life.

## Swati

*Symbol*: coral.
*Personal traits*: active, ambitious, full of ideas, disciplined, practical, risk-taker, good strategist or politician, can manipulate and play the power game, intelligent, idealistic, seeks wealth, does not always see his own limitations, wants to be the best, and is motivated by materialistic affairs *(artha)*. This star, which has the ability to adapt to the course of events, reflects disciplined energy, and gives the power and ability to influence others through communication.

## Vishakha • Saturn is exalted in Vishakha

*Symbol*: potter's wheel.
*Personal traits*: inwardly tormented, pleasure loving, larger than life personality, attracts admirers and friends, good adviser, ambitious, dissatisfied with material success, in search of the profound mysteries of nature, loves fashion, confident in facing obstacles, calm in a crisis, sober, and seeks virtue in action

*(dharma).* This star represents maturity acquired through experience, and it bestows the power to obtain a variety of different results in this life.

### Anuradha

*Symbol*: lotus.
*Personal traits*: oscillates between extremes: sometimes spiritual, sometimes materialistic, kind or cruel, happy or sad... Success will come when he finds the right balance. Feels overwhelmed, seeks excellence, lives in the future, intelligent, active, good adviser, tough, and seeks virtue in action *(dharma).* This star, like the lotus that blooms in stagnant water to be offered to the gods, bestows the power of devotion.

### Jyeshtha

*Symbol*: earring.
*Personal traits*: has the feeling that life is about change, wants to make a difference, interested in occult mysteries, determined, ambitious and possibly ready to step on others to reach his goals, highly intelligent, but fears losing his intuition, strength and power, disciplined, vulnerable to addictions, and motivated by strictly materialistic goals *(artha).* This star, which gives protection from danger, also gives the power to rise, conquer, and find courage in the midst of a battle.

### Mula

*Symbol*: lion-tail and elephant goad.
*Personal traits*: undergoes many great changes to which he adapts, explores the secrets of nature, the occult, and psychic energy, adventurous, brave, full of ideas, leader,

optimistic, cheerful, creates his own insecurities, will not slow down, disciplined, austere, and motivated by desire and passion, whether sexual, religious, for life, or for some cause *(kama).* This star, which evokes pain, anger, and abuse of power, yields the capacity to ruin, break, and destroy.

### Purvashadha

*Symbol*: elephant tusk.
*Personal traits*: creative, brilliant, talented, artistic, humble, victorious, changeable, periodically self-reinventing, seems misleading, attached to friends, and motivated by a quest for the highest degree of perfection *(moksha).* This star, which demonstrates that wisdom cannot be lost, just as a tusk will grow back if it is cut, also has the power to stimulate.

### Uttarashadha

*Symbol*: pallet.
*Personal traits*: dynamic, intellectual, leader, ambitious, brilliant, hates hypocrisy, fights corruption, may be fundamentalist or inflexible, very idealistic, but has difficulty accepting himself as he is or accepting others, lonely, and motivated by a quest for the highest degree of perfection *(moksha).* This star, which is symbolized by an austere bed where the mind can relax and open itself up to wisdom, gives one the power to conquer the unconquerable.

### Shravana

*Symbol*: ear.
*Personal traits*: very smart, brilliant even, very perceptive, loves silence, has peace of mind, knows how to

hear others, good politician and community leader, loves to serve others, compassionate, and motivated by physical activity (*artha*). This star, which bestows the ability to hear more than what is being said, gives the power to bond with others.

### Dhanishtha • Mars is exalted in Dhanishtha

*Symbol*: drum or flute.
*Personal traits*: has a great aptitude for spirituality even while living in the world, bright, charismatic, radiant, strong in thought, word and deed, leader, capable of self-sacrifice, knows when to speak and when to listen, has knowledge of the occult, needs to help others, may become a victim of others' ambitions, and emphasizes honesty and duty (*dharma*). This star's symbols indicate that it vibrates to someone else's rhythm, but remains empty inside; nevertheless, it has the power to provide abundance and glory.

### Shatabhisha

*Symbol*: a hundred stars.
*Personal traits*: able to accomplish the impossible, ambitious, highly perceptive, lacks confidence, needs to find happiness in himself and not in external accomplishments, needs to learn detachment, and seeks virtue in action (*dharma*). This star, which represents one's relationship with the cosmos and past karma, possesses the power of healing.

### Purva Bhadrapada

*Symbol*: sword or pen.
*Personal traits*: calm and placid as long as the question of injustice in the world is not raised, has strong

opinions, even prejudices, but is caring, good writer, very creative, needs to plan his finances, and is motivated by physical activity *(artha)*, which serves as a springboard to find answers in the cosmos. This star, whose symbol is an instrument used in the pursuit of an ideal or to protect the innocent, gives one the power to rise spiritually.

### Uttara Bhadrapada

*Symbol*: twins.
*Personal traits*: very wise, has a sense of destiny, detachment, seeks equality for all, idealistic, compassionate, charitable, benevolent, generous, a good teacher and advisor, not selfish. If negative: lazy and obese, prone to bad associations. Motivated by passion and the desire to help humanity *(kama)*. This star evokes the constant dualities between high and low, but also has the power to bring celestial rain, the source of fertility.

### Revati • Venus is exalted in Revati

*Symbol*: fish.
*Personal traits*: empathetic, caring, and sensitive to everyone, to the point that people try to take advantage of him, works quietly for the betterment of humanity, lacks self-confidence, beautiful, can feel like or become a victim, motivated by a quest for the highest degree of perfection, where the material ego ceases to exist *(moksha)*. This star's symbol is the best of good omens, as well as a guarantee of the happiness that comes from immersion in the ocean of the Absolute. It also has the power to feed and fulfill.

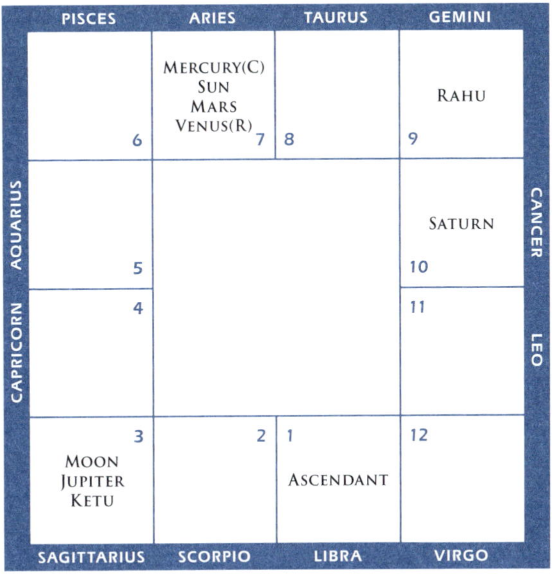
PISCES
ARIES
TAURUS
GEMINI
CANCER
LEO
VIRGO
LIBRA
SCORPIO
SAGITTARIUS
CAPRICORN
AQUARIUS
MERCURY(C)
SUN
MARS
VENUS(R)
RAHU
SATURN
MOON
JUPITER
KETU
ASCENDANT
1
2
3
4
5
6
7
8
9
10
11
12

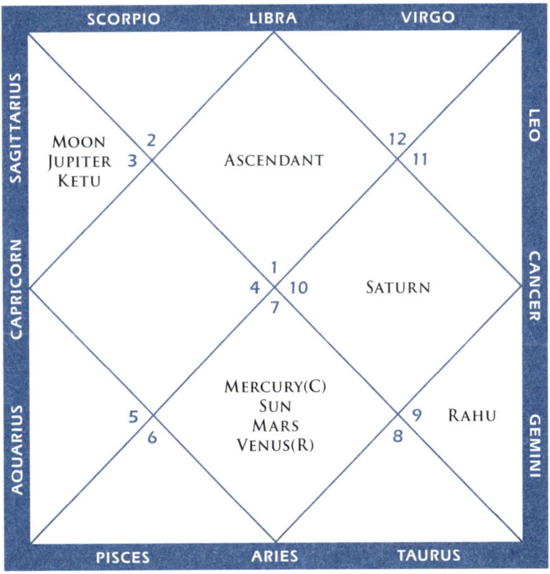
SCORPIO
LIBRA
VIRGO
LEO
CANCER
GEMINI
TAURUS
ARIES
PISCES
AQUARIUS
CAPRICORN
SAGITTARIUS
ASCENDANT
MOON
JUPITER
KETU
SATURN
MERCURY(C)
SUN
MARS
VENUS(R)
RAHU
1
2
3
4
5
6
7
8
9
10
11
12

Let us here take yet another look at Adolf Hitler.

We have here the degrees at which each planet is situated, so that we can tell which constellations have been activated by the planets. The lords of the constellations can be considered as secondary dispositors of the planets occupying them. For example, Mars is in *Bharani,* which has the power to clean and remove impurities, and obtains Venus, the lord of *Bharani* also in *Bharani,* as a secondary dispositor. Too bad the man tried to clean and remove impurities from society rather than from himself...

Table of degrees - Adolf Hitler

| | | | | | |
|---|---|---|---|---|---|
| Ascendant | 4°22′ | *Chitra* | Sun | 8°30′ | *Ashwini* |
| Moon | 14°19′ | *Purvashada* | Mars | 24°04′ | *Bharani* |
| Jupiter | 15°56′ | *Purvashada* | Venus | 24°23′ | *Bharani* |
| Ketu | 22°47′ | *Purvashada* | Rahu | 22°47′ | *Punarvasu* |
| Mercury | 3°21′ | *Ashwini* | Saturn | 21°09′ | *Ashlesha* |

## Exercise 4 – Exploring a Chart

### The Influence of the Constellations on Our Mystery Star

Let us apply the constellations in the study of the chart of our mystery star. We will not repeat all the meanings of each of the relevant constellations here, but only their power and their lord. Still, all the information that has been given will prove valuable and allow for a more detailed reading of the horoscope.

Moreover, since we have already observed the interactions of the natal chart's factors by and large, let us study the stars from the position of their ruler in the 9th division chart.

### ASCENDANT IN *HASTA*

The Ascendant in *Hasta* has the power to make what is sought a reality. It is governed by the Moon, which lies in Gemini in the 4th house of the 9th division. The sociable twins want to communicate, whereas house 4 is all about perceptions and emotions. We could thus say that our star can express and attain what she seeks by touching the heartstrings of her entourage. As *Hasta* is the star of the Ascendant, the importance of which we now know well, it testifies to our celebrity's success.

### SATURN IN *CHITRA*

Saturn in *Chitra* gives the power to accumulate merit in this life. It is governed by Mars in conjunction with Jupiter in the 10th house of the 9th division, in Sagittarius—a fire sign that aims as far and high as is possible. As Saturn is the planet of truth, the influence it receives from this powerful Jupiter gives it a surprising ambition and determination that the fire of Mars, the lord of house 9, can only further enkindle. Our mystery star has no doubt already accumulated a fortune, but this also suggests that she could reap other benefits that will only come to her in a future life.

### JUPITER IN *SWATI*

Jupiter in *Swati* provides the authority and ability to influence others through communication. It is governed by Rahu in the 5th house of the 9th division, in Cancer. The insatiable cravings of Rahu are expressed both in the sign of emotions and the house of the intellect. Rahu thus impels our star to exploit the realm of emotions in her work since Jupiter is posited in the 10th house of career in the 9th division. And, as we know, this professionally and commercially profitable artistic output is transmitted by radio, television, the Internet and other media.

### MERCURY IN *ANURADHA*

Mercury in *Anuradha* gives the power of devotion. It is governed by Saturn in Leo and in the 6th house of the 9th division. Mercury, the ruler of the Ascendant, is once again linked to Saturn through a star caught between two extremes, which blossoms to be offered to the gods like a young virgin to her future lover. The whole scene takes place in the sign of Leo, which loves to be a subject of adoration for others, and in the 6th house, that of ennemies. I'll let you decide if her admirers and the paparazzi are her true friends or not.

### SUN IN *ANURADHA*

The Sun in *Anuradha* gives the power of devotion. It is also governed by Saturn, just like Mercury. So this effectively confirms everything we have said about Mercury above and makes our star's ego subjected to love games both tender and cruel. We'll note that the Sun occupies Scorpio in both the natal and 9th division charts, which makes it much stronger. One problem with the Sun in water signs is the difficulty to shine through the wet stuff, i.e. emotions. This can lead to frustrations which pour out as emotional outbursts. But then, even this can be successfully commercialized!

### KETU IN *UTTARASHADHA*

Ketu in *Uttarashadha* gives the power to conquer the unconquerable. It is governed by the Sun in Scorpio in the 9th house of the 9th division. Ketu, in close contact

Table of degrees - Mystery star

| | | | | | |
|---|---|---|---|---|---|
| Ascendant | 9°47′ | *Uttara Phalguni* | Ketu | 1°09′ | *Uttarashadha* |
| Saturn | 25°40′ | *Chitra* | Venus | 1°30′ | *Uttarashadha* |
| Jupiter | 7°24′ | *Swati* | Moon | 18°47′ | *Shravana* |
| Sun | 11°49′ | *Anuradha* | Rahu | 1°09′ | *Punarvasu* |
| Mercury | 16°26′ | *Anuradha* | Mars | 29°40′ | *Uttara Phalguni* |

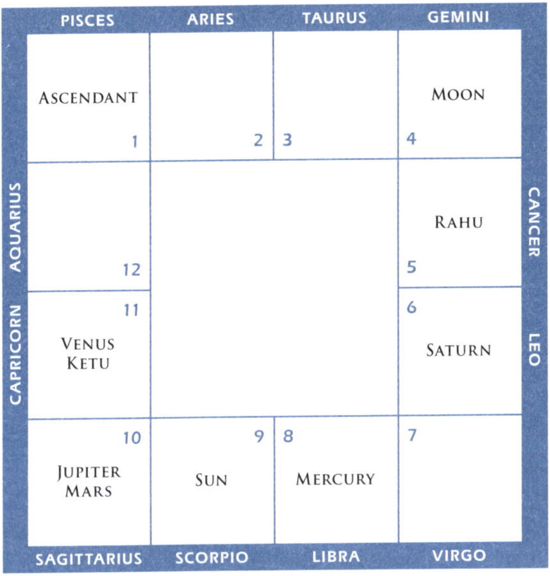


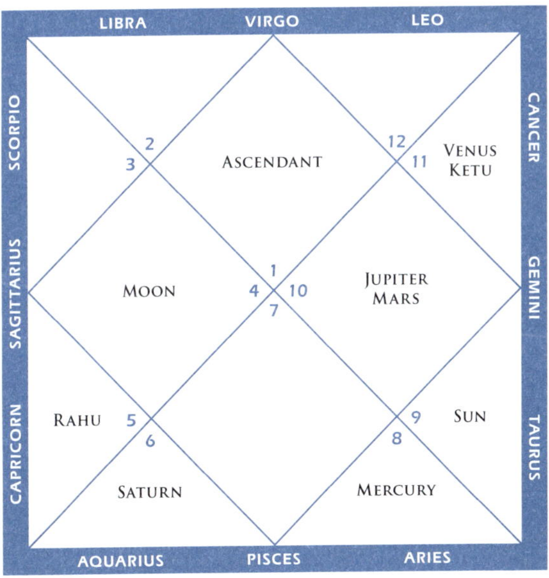


9th division — The influence of the constellations on our mystery star

with Venus, is also influenced by the sign of Scorpio, a secret sign, expressive of sexuality, which adds spice to Ketu and Venus for a great conquest of hearts, creating almost a religion among our star's followers.

### VENUS IN *UTTARASHADHA*

Venus in *Uttarashadha* gives the power to conquer the unconquerable. It is governed by the Sun, as is Ketu (well, well!). We can double the dose of what was said about Ketu and acclaim our star as a goddess with warm passions.

### MOON IN *SHRAVANA*

Moon in *Shravana* gives the ability to bond with others. It is governed by the Moon in Gemini in the 4th house of the 9th division. The sociable Gemini wants to communicate and loves marketing, whereas house 4 is one of perceptions and emotions. Let us mention once more that our mystery star makes a profitable use of all these houses and signs' meanings.

### RAHU IN *PUNARVASU*

Rahu in *Punarvasu* gives the power to obtain wealth and abundance. It is governed by Jupiter in Sagittarius in the 10th house of the 9th division. Need we say more? This beautiful star gives Rahu everything it needs to satisfy its desires and opulence equal to its ambitions. Success, wealth, and glory.

### MARS IN *UTTARA PHALGUNI*

Mars in *Uttara Phalguni* gives the power to acquire wealth through marriage. It is governed by the Sun in Scorpio in house 9 of the 9th division. This is an interesting one. Mars is doubly ruled by the Sun, which is lord of the house of losses in the natal chart and lord of the house of enemies in the 9th division. If prosperity equals media attention, alright. Otherwise, let us hope she finds a companion of quality who will also respect her. In the meantime, she's paying alimony (still $US 20,000 per month)!

You will note with interest that Jupiter and Rahu are connected through the exchange of their respective stars. This exchange between two planets of expansion, both located in money houses, is certainly one of the many factors indicating the financial success of the artist.

### Tips for Exploring Your Own Chart

The constellations occupied by the Ascendant and the different planets enrich and refine the significations we have already described. Here we spent time looking at the 9th division, but we could as easily have been studying the natal chart from other angles of vision. For example, since *Hasta,* the star of the Ascendant, is ruled by the Moon, there is another link between it and Saturn, which is found in the Ascendant, and as we have seen previously, this combination may cause depression.

It will certainly be useful to check where the lords of your constellations are posited in your birth chart. If you notice that the same planet governs several of your constellations, its influence will be increased.

# PLANETARY COMBINATIONS

In Vedic astrology, the word "yoga" (union) refers to a combination of specific factors that, taken together, reveal much more than the position of an individual planet in a sign or a house. Moreover, many Vedic astrologers undertake the first review of a chart by analyzing the number of yogas in it and their strength. This examination makes it possible to assess an individual's potential for achievement, which may surpass the usual criteria of human experience when benefic yogas are present, or conversely be hindered by to great difficulties in the presence of malefic yogas.

The yogas referred to, which are formed by special planetary arrangements, produce specific results and may involve:

- Planets alone;
- Planets and houses;
- Planets and signs; or
- Some combination of planet, house, and sign.

The effects of any yoga are modified by the general condition of the sign and the house in which it is formed. Thus, a benefic yoga will not produce the same results in a hidden house as it would in a powerful quadrant. The dispositor of the house in which the yoga occurs must also be well situated for it to fully produce its effects.

All yogas will also be modified by their conjunctions with one or more planets and aspects received from other planets. Furthermore, we must consider the proximity of the Sun, as a combusted planet weakens a yoga.

Since there are hundreds of yogas, we will just cover some of the main ones here:

- Yogas of greatness;
- Royal yogas, indicative of success;
- Yogas of financial prosperity;
- Yogas of difficulty and suffering;
- Lunar yogas;
- Solar yogas;
- Yogas where two lords exchange signs;
- Yogas where lords of hidden houses exchange places;
- Yogas resulting from the cancellation of a planet's debilitation;
- Yogas of the Ascendant;
- The elephant-lion yoga, which bestows authority, strength, and power; and
- The karmic snake yoga.

Important note: The aspects we will consider for the formation of yogas are here limited to the planets, and those of the signs will be pushed into the background. Where applicable, we will also consider yogas from the Sun's position, which will come in useful in our next chapter.

To know whether a yoga is manifesting strongly, we must verify whether:

- The planets involved are in a trine (houses 5 and 9) from the Ascendant or the Moon, and associated with benefics that are not combust;

- The planets involved are related to the Ascendant;
- The yoga from the Ascendant is also present from the position of the Moon; and
- The native will go through the periods of influence of the planets involved in the yoga during the productive years of his life, i.e., between 20 and 60, rather than in childhood or old age.

Let's now dive headfirst into the yogas, starting with...

## Yogas of Greatness

Yogas of greatness arise when a planet occupies its own sign or exaltation sign in a quadrant of either the natal or Moon charts. Only Mars, Mercury, Jupiter, Venus, and Saturn can form such yogas. Needless to say, these yogas only manifest their higher nature fully when they receive benefic aspects.

### *Ruchaka Yoga*

Mars in Aries, Scorpio, or Capricorn in a quadrant. The power of Mars will dominate and the native will be energetic, adventurous, and discerning. A beneficial aspect on Mars will enhance the potential of this yoga, while a malefic aspect might arouse anger and violence. The native will often be physically strong and love sports in general, but especially those related to combat and martial arts. Often very intelligent, graduate studies suit him well. This yoga, whose keywords are "sharp" and "radiant," may bring resounding success or stir up great cruelty. It can also occur when the Ascendant is in another movable or fixed sign—Cancer, Libra, Taurus, Leo, or Aquarius.

EXAMPLE: MUHAMMAD ALI

We see here that the Ascendant is in Cancer and Mars occupies Aries in house 10. In addition, Mars occupies the 4th house from the position of the Moon. As with all yogas, *Ruchaka* acquires more force when it is repeated in both the natal and Moon charts. No naturally benefic planet aspects Mars, but Mars is in conjunction with retrograde Saturn. Mr. Ali certainly showed his love and exceptional talent for boxing, becoming three times world champion. Saturn may have caused him problems and delays here and there, but it also gave him discipline and tenacity.

This yoga is even more powerful since Mars itself creates a royal yoga for a Cancer Ascendant. Moreover, Mars cancels Saturn's fall and creates another royal yoga by association. Finally, Mars is at its maximum strength when it occupies the 10th house, as is the case here.

## Bhadra Yoga

Mercury in Gemini or Virgo in a quadrant. This yoga gives one exceptional management and business skills. But the native, whose intelligence is very bright, will also be particularly good at studies and well equipped to brilliantly exercise his talents as a creator, writer, and communicator. Because Mercury is easily influenced by other planets, this yoga can bring success in almost any area. It can, however, only occur when the Ascendant is in a movable sign.

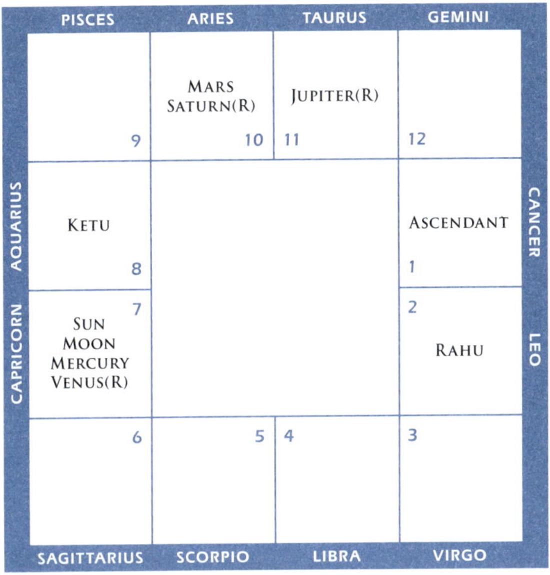
PISCES
ARIES
TAURUS
GEMINI
9
MARS
SATURN(R)
10
JUPITER(R)
11
12
AQUARIUS
KETU
8
CANCER
ASCENDANT
1
CAPRICORN
7
SUN
MOON
MERCURY
VENUS(R)
LEO
2
RAHU
6
5
4
3
SAGITTARIUS
SCORPIO
LIBRA
VIRGO

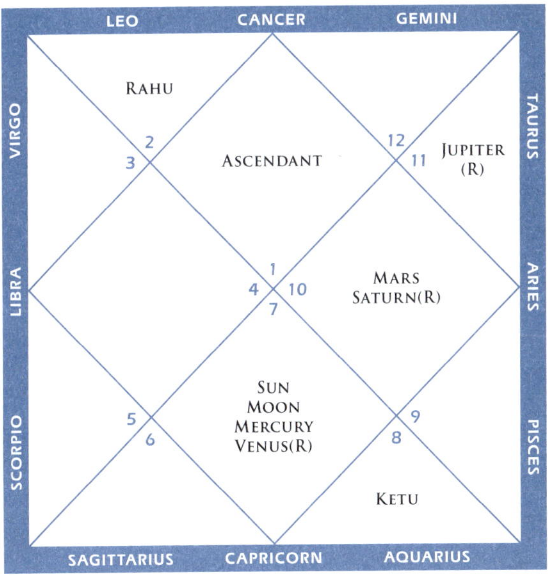
LEO
CANCER
GEMINI
RAHU
VIRGO
2
3
ASCENDANT
12
11
JUPITER
(R)
TAURUS
LIBRA
1
4
10
7
MARS
SATURN(R)
ARIES
SCORPIO
5
6
SUN
MOON
MERCURY
VENUS(R)
9
8
KETU
PISCES
SAGITTARIUS
CAPRICORN
AQUARIUS

Bhadra yoga – Bill Gates

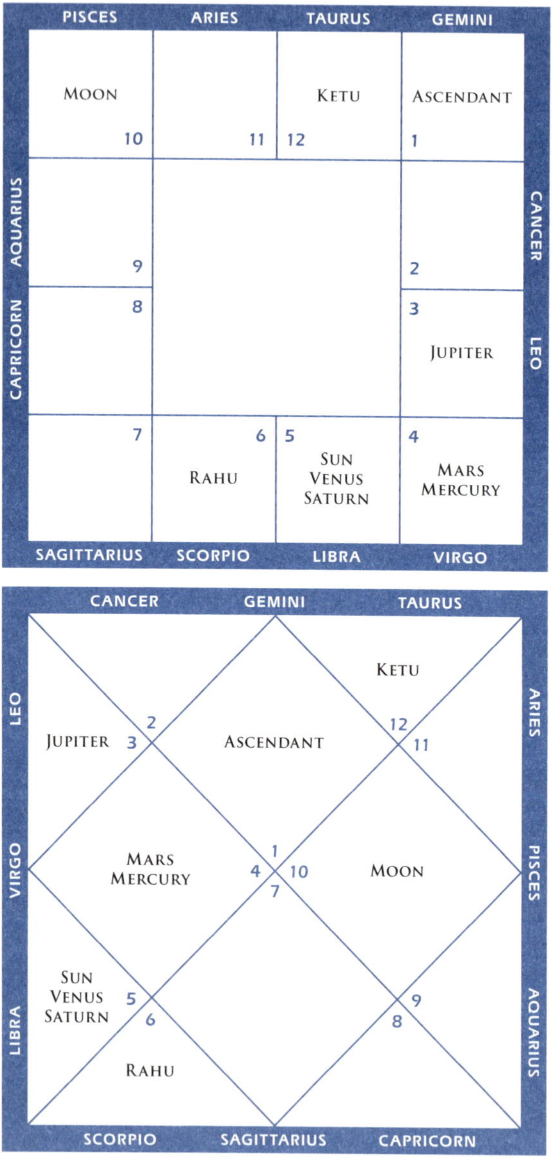

EXAMPLE: BILL GATES

Here is another look at the chart of Bill Gates, the man whose wealth we would all like to share! His Ascendant is in Gemini, whose lord is Mercury. Mercury is located in the 4th house, in its sign of exaltation, Virgo. It is also in the 7th house from the Moon, meaning that the benefic waxing Moon aspects it, which gives even more power to this yoga. Moreover, Mars is in conjunction with Mercury, which gives Mr. Gates an all-consuming energy while stimulating his intelligence and increasing his resources as well as his income, enemies and potential for litigations.

## Hamsa Yoga

Jupiter in Sagittarius, Pisces, or Cancer in a quadrant. *Hamsa* means a swan, the graceful bird that carries many of the heavenly deities in Vedic mythology. The native will have a nice face, a phlegmatic nature, and he will be like a king, verily respected by good people. He will relish delicious food and be virtuous. This yoga also arouses sexual passions.

EXAMPLE: PAUL NEWMAN

Jupiter occupies its own sign, Sagittarius, in the Ascendant. The yoga is not reproduced in the Moon chart, except that Mercury and Venus also occupy the Ascendant and bathe Jupiter with their benevolent energy even as they create other beneficial yogas. Also take note here of the aspect of Saturn, which necessarily creates some irritations, such as delays or the need to make some additional effort, even as it provides a structured mind and a healthy sobriety.

Hamsa yoga – Paul Newman

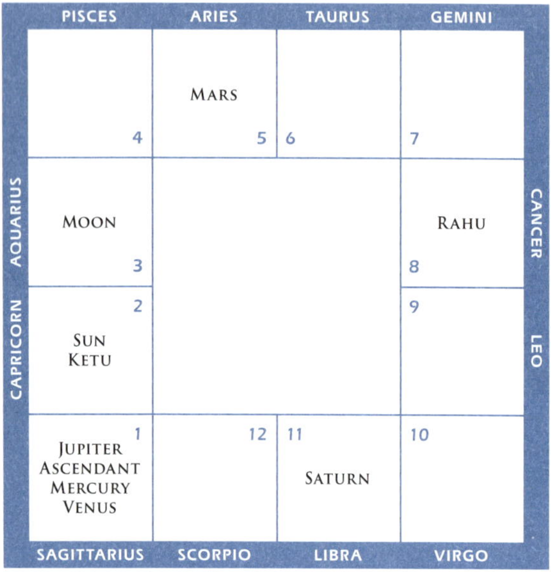


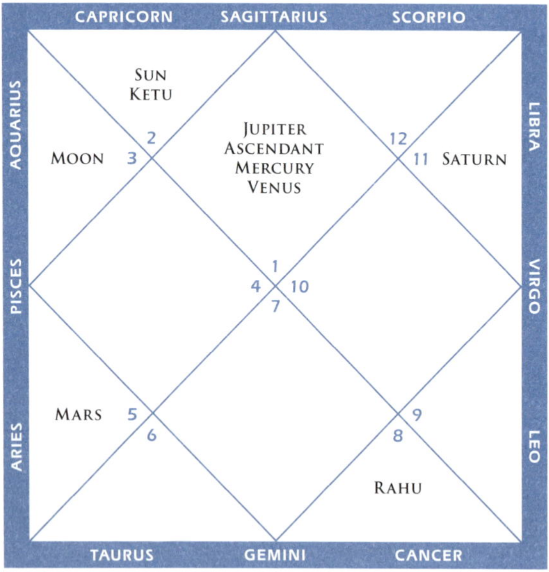

## Malavya Yoga

Venus in Taurus, Libra, or Pisces in a quadrant. This yoga is the full expression of pleasure. The native will be beautiful and will love beauty, money, and luxury. This yoga brings happiness, wealth, talent, and joy with family. It can be found with any Ascendant.

EXAMPLE: PRINCESS DIANA

The Ascendant is in Scorpio. Venus, in Taurus, occupies the 7th house of the natal chart and the 4th house from the Moon, which reproduces and reinforces the yoga. Venus is also receiving an aspect of Jupiter, which increases its power. Who would deny that Diana lived the life of a princess? The trouble with Venus in the 7th house is that it highlights the possibility of multiple love relationships that, let's face it, can interfere with family life, especially for a high-profile princess.

## Shasha Yoga

Saturn in Capricorn, Aquarius, or Libra, in a quadrant. This yoga produces individuals focused on their goals but at the same time detached, in other words, good leaders. Saturn is the planet of people, and the native is often drawn to politics. He will be competent, rich, and healthy and will have people serving him. He is good at science, also, but has a tendency to flirt with other people's wives. This yoga can also occur when the Ascendant occupies another mobile or fixed sign, such as Aries, Cancer, Taurus, Leo, or Scorpio.

EXAMPLE: WOODY ALLEN

Saturn occupies the sign of Aquarius in the 7th house of the natal chart and is in conjunction with the Moon, which doubly reinforces this yoga. Mr. Allen writes

Malavya yoga – Princess Diana

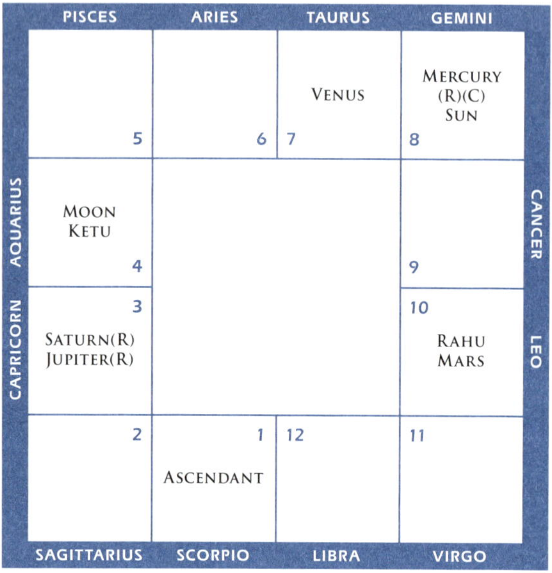


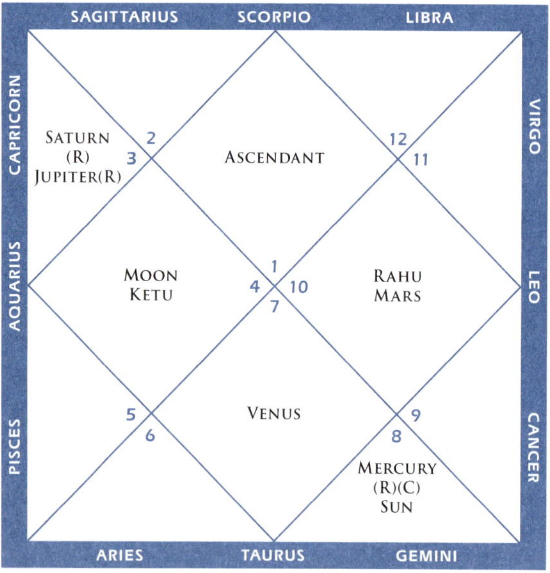

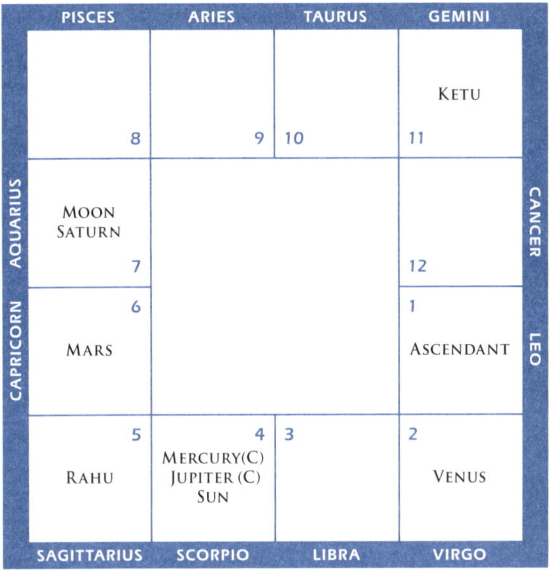


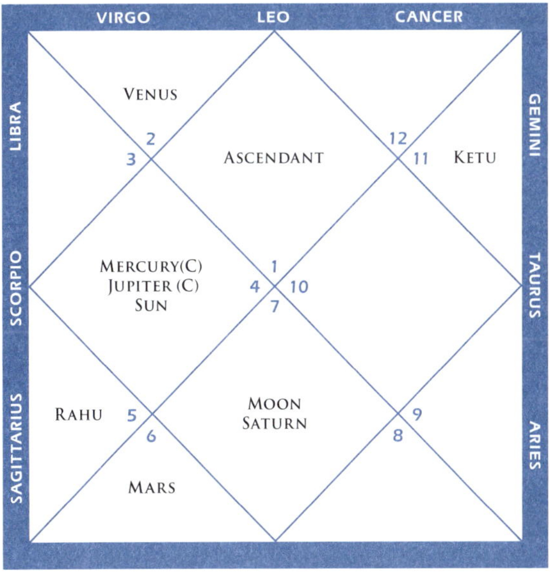


Sasha yoga – Woody Allen

and directs his own films, and well personifies the eccentricity often associated with Aquarius through his cynical yet philosophical persona. He even departed somewhat from the "flirt with other people's wives" by opting for his wife's daughter—eccentricity has its own ways.

## Royal Yogas

These yogas grant power, authority, and wealth when several are present in a chart, while a single one can give dignity or presence. People with such yogas rise materially in life without forgetting where they came from: their country, family status, situation, etc. They generally do better than others from the same milieu who do not have these yogas. The royal yogas favour those aspects of life that correspond to their position in a chart.

Since there are hundreds of royal yogas, we will here only look at those that are most easily identifiable, which are formed when the lord of a quadrant is associated with the ruler of a trine, or when the lords of trines are associated with each other. These yogas can manifest themselves in several ways:

- ❖ When the rulers are in conjunction in the same house. For example, for a Taurus Ascendant, the lord of house 5 is Mercury and Saturn is the lord of house 10. A royal yoga will be formed if they occupy the same sign or the same house.

- ❖ When lords mutually aspect one another. For example, for a Taurus Ascendant,

Mercury, the ruler of house 5 is in Leo, the 4th house, and Saturn, lord of the 10th house occupies the sign of Aquarius in house 10. The two planets are opposite each other and aspect each other, which creates a relationship between the two.

- Another yoga we would all like to see in our chart results from the union of the lords of trines, those houses of knowledge and progress that bring good fortune to our lives.

The quadrants being the houses of power, they benefit from a connection with the trines, which make circumstances most conducive for them. The most powerful royal yoga is formed when the lord of house 9 is linked to the lord of house 10.

For some Ascendants, a single planet, if simultaneously lord of a quadrant and a trine other than the Ascendant, may in itself form a royal yoga, no matter where it is located in the chart. Only three planets have access to this status. Here are the Ascendants that could give rise to such a yoga:

- Taurus Ascendant - Saturn governs houses 9 and 10;

- Libra Ascendant - Saturn governs houses 4 and 5;

- Cancer Ascendant - Mars rules houses 5 and 10;

- Leo Ascendant - Mars rules houses 4 and 9;

- ❖ Capricorn Ascendant - Venus governs houses 5 and 10;

- ❖ Aquarius Ascendant - Venus governs houses 4 and 9.

For these Ascendants, when the planet in question is well located and aspected, it can produce excellent results. If it is afflicted, the benefits will not be significant. Moreover, as Saturn and Mars are natural malefics, even when they do uplift the native, they do not do so without also providing obstacles to overcome.

EXAMPLE: JUSTIN TIMBERLAKE

In this chart we have a Leo Ascendant, where Mars governs houses 4 and 9, while being itself situated in Aquarius in the 7th house—a first royal yoga. Then, Jupiter, lord of the 5th, and Saturn, lord of the 7th, are in conjunction in house 2—a second royal yoga. Then Venus, lord of house 10, is in conjunction with the Sun, ruler of the Ascendant, in the 6th, which is the house of competitions—a third royal yoga. Note here that Venus, the planet of artists, also governs house 3, the house of the arts, and its presence alongside the Sun is indicative of Mr. Timberlake's artistic nature and the direction of his career.

## Yogas of Financial Prosperity

These wealth-indicating yogas result from the following configurations:

- ❖ The lord of house 5 or 9 is in conjunction with or mutually aspects the ruler(s) of the money houses (2 and 11).

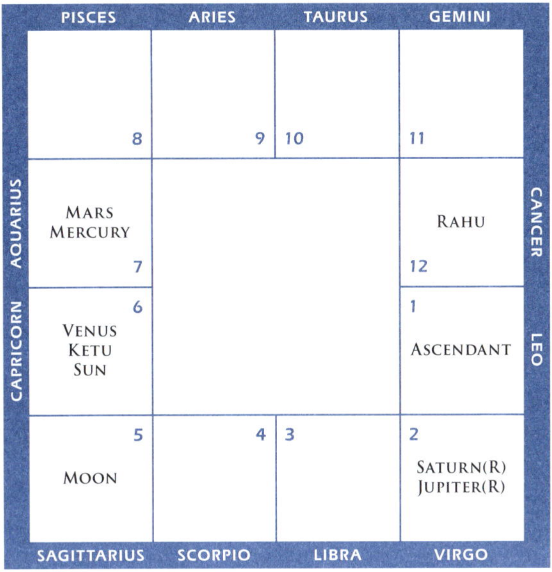
PISCES
ARIES
TAURUS
GEMINI
AQUARIUS
CAPRICORN
CANCER
LEO
SAGITTARIUS
SCORPIO
LIBRA
VIRGO
8
9
10
11
MARS
MERCURY
7
RAHU
12
6
VENUS
KETU
SUN
1
ASCENDANT
5
MOON
4
3
2
SATURN(R)
JUPITER(R)

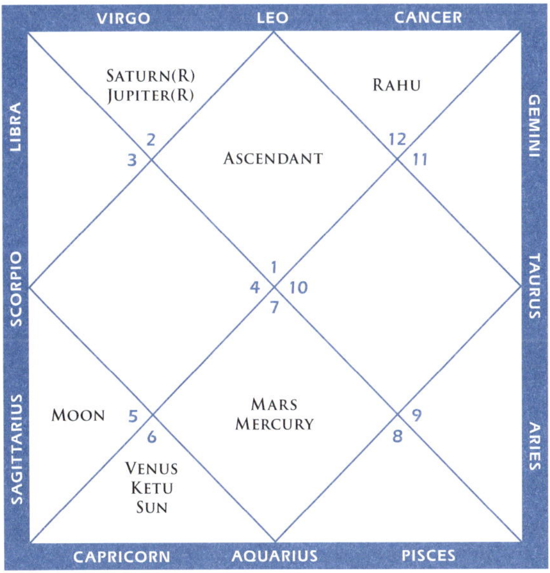
VIRGO
LEO
CANCER
LIBRA
SCORPIO
SAGITTARIUS
GEMINI
TAURUS
ARIES
CAPRICORN
AQUARIUS
PISCES
SATURN(R)
JUPITER(R)
2
3
RAHU
12
11
ASCENDANT
1
4
10
7
MOON
5
6
VENUS
KETU
SUN
MARS
MERCURY
9
8

- The lords of the trines mutually aspect each other.

- The ruler of a money house is in conjunction or in mutual aspect with the ruler of the Ascendant.

- The ruler of house 9 is in a quadrant or a trine, in its own sign or in its sign of exaltation, while the ruler of the Ascendant is strong (even stronger if the ruler of the 9th house or the Ascendant is connected with the ruler of a money house).

- A natural benefic occupies house 2 and receives no malefic aspect.

- A conjunction or mutual aspect of the Moon and Mars (especially if these planets are very powerful and connected to money houses). The wealth coming from this yoga is not necessarily from a legitimate source.

## Yogas of Difficulty and Suffering

These yogas are indicative of disease and mental instability. They bring misfortune, bad luck, and loss. They can also cause depression and general malaise. They may however be countered by more positive yogas, a strong Ascendant, and a well-placed lord of the Ascendant. For such yogas, the lords of houses 6, 8, or 12 must be in conjunction or in mutual aspect, and have an influence over house 1 or its ruler, or either the Moon or Sun. The more positive elements aspect such yogas, the less troubling their effects.

## Lunar Yogas

- One or more planets (except for the Sun, Rahu, and Ketu) occupy the 2nd house of the Moon chart. A natural benefic here may make the native rich and cultivated, or put him in a position of authority, whereas a natural malefic may be a source of challenges and difficulties.

- One or more planets (except for the Sun, Rahu, and Ketu) in the 12th house of the Moon chart will lead to financial gain, prosperity, and wealth.

- One or more planets (except for the Sun, Rahu, and Ketu) occupy houses 2 and 12 of the Moon chart. Benefics will provide wealth and power, while malefics will cause troubles and setbacks.

- No planets occupy the houses on either side of the Moon—lonely Moon—(excluding the Sun, Rahu, and Ketu). Leads to poverty, isolation, and the weakening of judgement and psychological balance. The presence of planets in the quadrants of the Moon chart cancels this yoga, as does the presence of the Moon in one of the quadrants or its conjunction with another planet. On the other hand, the effects of this yoga are rather more pronounced if the Moon occupies houses 6, 8, or 12.

- Jupiter, Venus, and Mercury occupy houses 6, 7, and 8 of the Moon chart: health, wealth, and social status.

## Solar Yogas

- One or more benefics (except for the Moon) occupy house 2 of the Sun chart: beauty, happiness, and prosperity.
- One or more planets (except for the Moon, Rahu, and Ketu) occupy house 12 of the Sun chart: a benefic indicates material gain and eloquence, whereas a malefic brings both difficulties and spiritual inclinations.
- One or more planets (except for the Moon, Rahu, and Ketu) occupy houses 2 and 12 of the Sun chart: if benefic, they indicate gains, if malefic, they bring difficulties.
- Mercury and the Sun conjoined in the same house bring intelligence and eloquence. This yoga is very common, but is all the same best strengthened by the conjunction or aspect of a benefic. Finally, a combust Mercury will improve intelligence, but not bestow eloquence.

## Yogas Where Two Lords Exchange Signs

Two planets are in an exchange of signs where they respectively occupy each other's houses, as for example if Venus is in Aries and Mars in Libra. All in all, there are 66 possible exchanges of this kind. This yoga is naturally beneficial when the exchange occurs between lords of two positive houses, but also when it occurs between the rulers of two negative houses, as the planets involved can then function as if in their own sign. On the other hand, this yoga is eminently malefic when the exchange occurs between the lord of a good house and that of a bad one, because the influence of the hidden houses will disturb important aspects of life, according to the houses involved.

## Yogas Where Lords of Hidden Houses Exchange Places

If the lord of a hidden house (6, 8, or 12) is situated in one of the hidden houses other than his own, or makes a trade with another ruler of such a house, this indicates happiness, gain, fame, and conquest over difficulties. Such yogas are strengthened when the planets occupy their sign of exaltation.

## Yogas Resulting From the Cancellation of a Planet's Debilitation

A debilitated planet can see its condition changed or reversed. Such a planet usually produces adverse effects in early life which can however be reversed in time, and even give rise to royal yogas. The cancellation of a planet's fall or debilitation occurs when:

- The debilitated planet occupies a quadrant in the natal or Moon chart, including the Ascendant, or is in conjunction with the Moon.

- The debilitated planet is exalted in the 9th division.
- The lord of either the sign of exaltation or of fall of the planet in question occupies a quadrant in the natal or Moon chart (if Mars is in Cancer, the Moon or Saturn must be in a quadrant).
- The debilitated planet is either connected to its dispositor, or in either conjunction or mutual aspect with the ruler of its sign of exaltation.
- The debilitated planet is in conjunction with an exalted planet.
- Two debilitated planets occupy each other's sign.

EXAMPLE: ALBERT EINSTEIN

In his chart, Einstein has:

- A yoga of greatness (*Malavya*), three royal yogas, a yoga of prosperity with the lords of houses 1, 5, and 9, and one solar yoga.
- Another royal yoga between the lords of houses 9 and 10.
- An elephant-lion yoga (described below).
- A yoga linking hidden houses with Mars, lord of house 6 in exaltation in the 8th.
- A yoga resulting from the cancellation of Mercury's debilitation by Venus, which is exalted in a quadrant.

Yogas — Albert Einstein

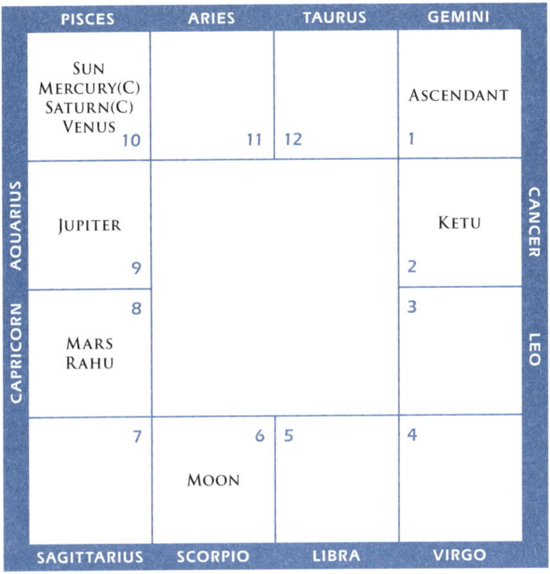


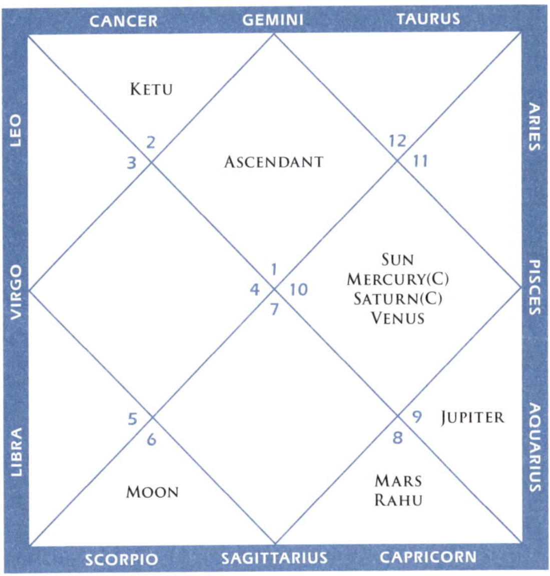

- A lunar yoga of lonely Moon.

- Yogas of difficulty and suffering: Venus lord of the 12th and Saturn lord of the 8th are conjunct with the Ascendant lord.

Since the numerous planets creating favourable yogas in Einstein's chart are connected to the 10th house and the lord of the Ascendant, either directly or indirectly through Saturn, it goes without saying that our man has become famous for his work. He also had to bear the brunt of his yogas of suffering as when he was only 15, his family went bankrupt and moved to Italy, leaving him alone in Munich to complete his studies. This is not to mention the two destabilizing world wars he lived through in Europe, his two marriages, and the deep regret he felt for having contributed to the creation of the first great weapon of mass destruction. There is always a price to pay for fame!

## Yogas of the Ascendant

The sage Parashara decreed that the presence of Jupiter in the Ascendant compensates for many flaws. Still, some other combinations can be either favourable or unfavourable.

- *Favourable combinations*: natural benefics in houses 2 or 12 lead to longevity, health, happiness, and wealth.

- *Unfavourable combinations*: natural malefics in houses 2 or 12 lead to short life, poverty, impurity, loneliness, unhappiness, celibacy.

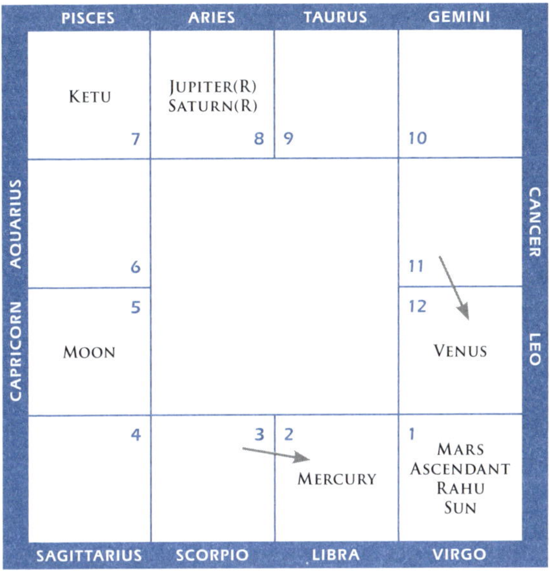
PISCES
ARIES
TAURUS
GEMINI
KETU
7
JUPITER(R)
SATURN(R)
8
9
10
AQUARIUS
6
11
CANCER
CAPRICORN
5
MOON
12
VENUS
LEO
4
3
2
MERCURY
1
MARS
ASCENDANT
RAHU
SUN
SAGITTARIUS
SCORPIO
LIBRA
VIRGO

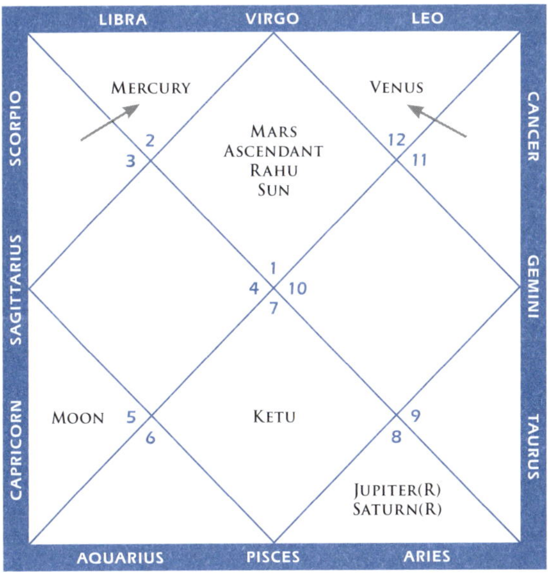
LIBRA
VIRGO
LEO
SCORPIO
MERCURY
VENUS
CANCER
2
3
MARS
ASCENDANT
RAHU
SUN
12
11
SAGITTARIUS
1
4
10
7
GEMINI
CAPRICORN
MOON
5
6
KETU
9
8
TAURUS
JUPITER(R)
SATURN(R)
AQUARIUS
PISCES
ARIES

EXAMPLE: JOHN LENNON

The houses that surround the Virgo Ascendant are both occupied by natural benefics, namely Jupiter and Mercury. As we know, Mr. Lennon had health, wealth, and happiness. The three malefics in the Ascendant, however, reduced his longevity.

## The Elephant-Lion Yoga

The Moon in conjunction with Jupiter or in houses 4, 7, or 10 from Jupiter leads to power, leadership, wealth, and the ability to defeat one's enemies.

## The Karmic Snake Yoga

This yoga is formed when all the planets are situated on the same side of the chart between Rahu and Ketu. It is said that they are then "swallowed" by the lunar nodes and this results in many unexpected reversals. For example, if all the planets are to one side of houses 1 and 7, one's married life may be affected, while to one side of houses 4 and 10, it could cause one's career to suffer. This yoga could indicate a narrow-minded person who sees everything in black and white and who usually needs to repeat the same mistakes several times before he can embrace change. Such a person will be very focused on his goals and can probably attain them, but not without difficulties.

EXAMPLE: DONALD TRUMP

In this chart, the karmic snake yoga is formed on the axis of houses 5 and 11, signifying investments. Trump

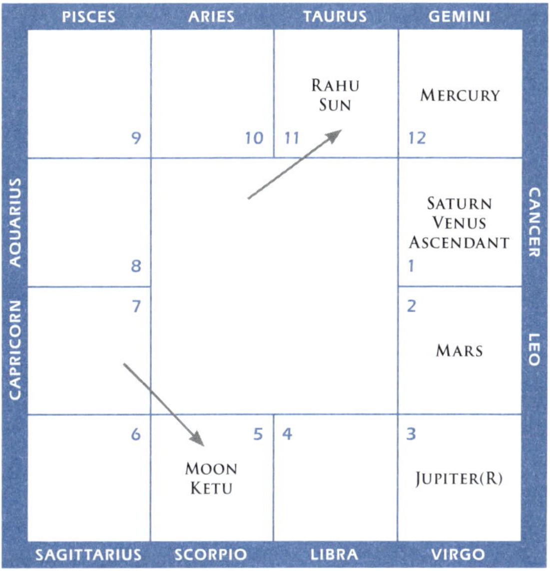


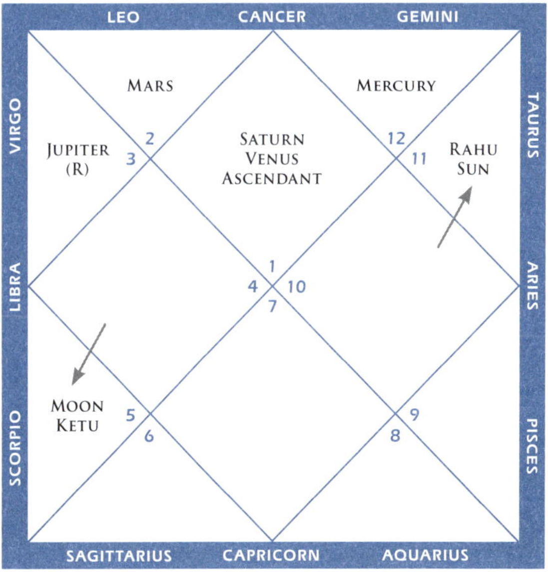


Karmic snake yoga — Donald Trump

won, lost, and regained billions of dollars in his business ventures. This yoga is even more marked in his case because he was born on the day of an eclipse, when the lunar nodes dominate one of the luminaries, a situation which confers Mr. Trump an unusual type of ego (you'll agree).

## Exercise 5 – Exploring a Chart

### The Yogas That Influence Our Mystery Star

#### ROYAL YOGAS

In our star's Moon chart (where the position of the Moon corresponds to the Ascendant, i.e., house 1):

- Venus who is simultaneously lord of houses 5 and 10, confers power.
- Venus is in conjunction with the Moon, lord of the 7th house, which accentuates the importance of the public and business partnerships.

In the Sun chart (where the Sun's position corresponds to the Ascendant):

- The combination of Ketu, the ruler of Scorpio, with the Moon, ruler of house 9, creates two types of royal yogas, since Scorpio is here both a quadrant and a trine. The result is a harmony between the two houses of *dharma*, reflecting the achievements of our star in the world by artfully using communication and emotions.

- ❖ The conjunction of Ketu, lord of house 1, with Venus, lord of the 7th, indicates that both love and business relationships are important for our star.

- ❖ The conjunction of Venus, lord of the 7th house, with the Moon, lord of the 9th, also highlights the relationships indicated by the 7th house, and shows that our star benefits from some of them.

### PROSPERITY YOGAS

The conjunction of Venus, lord of houses 2 and 9, with the Moon, lord of house 11 in the 5th and in Capricorn, the sign of career, is indicative of relentless hard work. We have already discussed this combination earlier, and the fact that it forms a yoga amplifies the ability of each participating planet to further garnish our celebrity's bank account.

In the Moon chart:

- ❖ Rahu, ruler of Aquarius—house 2—is in mutual aspect with Ketu, ruler of the 11th, as well as Venus, ruler of the 5th. This yoga is made all the more powerful since the lunar nodes occupy the same degree as Venus ($US 120 million, I believe, was the figure mentioned...).

- ❖ Jupiter in the 2nd house, without any malefic aspect, promises important income as a quadrant lord.

In the Sun chart:

- Jupiter, which governs houses 2 and 5, is in the 12th house, meaning money from abroad.

- In addition, we will remember that Jupiter is related to Rahu by their respective stars, which creates a further relationship between houses 2, 5, and 9 from the solar Ascendant and houses 2 and 11 from the regular Ascendant.

#### YOGAS OF DIFFICULTY AND SUFFERING

The Ascendant lord Mercury is with the Sun, the 12th lord, and aspected by Mars, the 8th lord (in sign exchange with the Sun), as well as by Saturn, the 6th lord. So yes, this confirms suffering due to mental instability which is likely to bring misfortune, bad luck and loss, depression and general malaise when our star is subjected to acute spells.

#### YOGAS WHERE LORDS OF HIDDEN HOUSES EXCHANGE PLACES

Mars, ruler of the 8th, occupies the 12th house while the Sun—the 12th lord—is in Scorpio in house 3, which allows our star to overcome obstacles and emerge victorious despite the fact that this also creates a yoga of difficulty and suffering (relief!)

#### SOLAR YOGAS

- Jupiter in the 12th house of the Sun chart—income.

- The conjunction of the Sun and Mercury in the 3rd house brings intelligence, all the

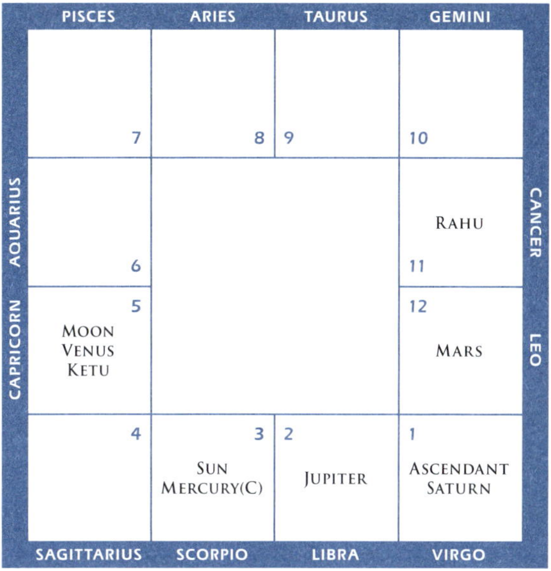
PISCES
ARIES
TAURUS
GEMINI
7
8
9
10
AQUARIUS
6
RAHU
11
CANCER
CAPRICORN
5
MOON
VENUS
KETU
12
MARS
LEO
4
3
SUN
MERCURY(C)
2
JUPITER
1
ASCENDANT
SATURN
SAGITTARIUS
SCORPIO
LIBRA
VIRGO

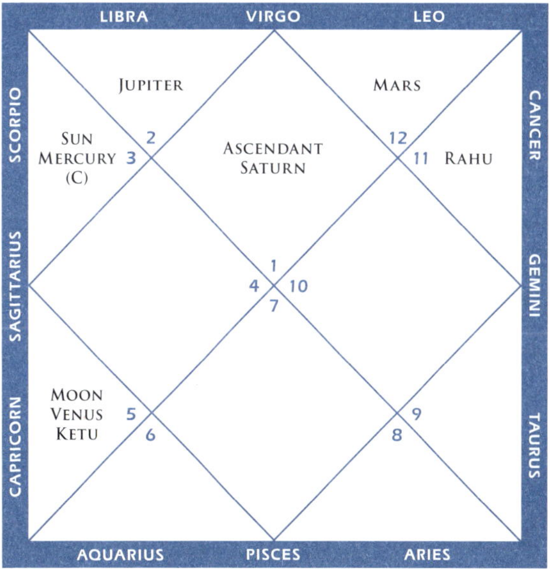
LIBRA
VIRGO
LEO
JUPITER
MARS
SCORPIO
SUN
MERCURY
(C)
3
2
ASCENDANT
SATURN
12
11
RAHU
CANCER
SAGITTARIUS
1
4
10
7
GEMINI
CAPRICORN
MOON
VENUS
KETU
5
6
9
8
TAURUS
AQUARIUS
PISCES
ARIES

more so as Ketu in house 5 embraces two benefics… while being very much afflicted by all the malefics of the chart, suggesting that this intelligence is used for trivial purposes.

ELEPHANT-LION YOGA

Jupiter in Libra is 10 houses away from the Moon in Capricorn, and vice versa: leadership, fortune, and victory over one's enemies. This yoga gives our celebrity even more importance and visibility since the conjunction in Capricorn benefits from it. Hence the possibility of being in contact with powerful people possessing a certain amount of wisdom and proficiency in regard to money and pleasure. Jupiter connects houses 2 and 5 from the Ascendant (money), 1 and 10 in the Moon chart (career), and 3 and 12 in the Sun chart (international artist).

As we can see, even with a natal chart as difficult as this one, the artist has several yogas of prosperity to her credit. The lunar nodes are also very powerful. In addition, each planet activates the other yogas in which it participates. Nice teamwork.

In fact, our artist was an accomplished gymnast in her youth, participating in various competitions in her home state until the age of 9. She then took part in many artistic productions in New York, and at the age of 11, landed a role on the Disney Channel, and then in a popular television series at 12.

During her career as a singer, dancer, actress, and songwriter, she has so far sold over 133 million records worldwide, and has for many years been the most sought after person on Google. And you can be sure that the paparazzi, which we can associate with house 3 for communications and the parasitic quality of the lunar nodes, await her at every turn.

### Tips for Exploring Your Own Chart

Now it is your turn to identify the yogas present in your chart. This exercise is especially gratifying in that it will help you crystallize the trends shown by the general structure of your horoscope.

Any positive yoga involving the lord of your Ascendant will certainly enhance your personal success to the extent that the planets involved occupy favourable signs. Such a yoga will grant results according to the house or houses where it occurs. For example, in the 1st house, the native himself shines; in the 2nd, financial benefits prevail; in the 3rd, it is creativity and communication, and so on. Any yoga formed in a quadrant will play a leading role in your life, sometimes acting on your health, or on the quality of your home or car, your professional life, or the success or failure of your business.

So far, we have gone through several steps in the analysis of a chart, and we now know that the planets provide us with an incredible amount of information through their position, their interactions, the signs and astrological houses they occupy, as well as through the special combinations to which they give rise, not to mention the constellations and their influence. Let us now turn to the times when such influences are most likely to occur.

# Chapter 6

# PLANETARY PERIODS

## Slices of Life – The Case of Albert Einstein

Everything we've seen so far concerns the static interpretation of an astrological chart and is based on the birth coordinates, which provide a snapshot of the native's karma at that precise moment. However, the same chart must also be considered dynamically, that is to say, taking into account the periods of influence and current position of each planet. We will then see that trends identified in the chart become particularly evident when the planets in question are fully active.

Regarding the planetary periods, the *vimshottari* system of sage Parashara is the most widely used because it generally gives the best results, even though there are several other systems which allow one to seek a second opinion—Parashara himself elaborates on 42!

The *vimshottari* system describes the major periods during which each planet exerts a dominant influence, and minor periods, where each planet takes its turn modulating the effects of the dominant planet governing that particular slice of one's life. This allows us to predict future events and target appropriate times for certain undertakings, keeping in mind that each individual has free will to make his own decisions and choose his own attitudes.

The system of Parashara that we follow here spans 120 years, which gives ample time for even the strongest

The influence of planetary periods on Albert Einstein

| **Mercury** (17 years) From 0 years to 9.8 years | | |
|---|---|---|
| Sub-period | Start | End |
| Mercury | | |
| Ketu | | |
| Venus | | |
| Sun | | |
| Moon | 03-14-1879 | 05-15-1880 |
| Mars | 05-15-1880 | 05-13-1881 |
| Rahu | 05-13-1881 | 11-30-1883 |
| Jupiter | 11-30-1883 | 03-07-1886 |
| Saturn | 03-07-1886 | 11-14-1888 |

| **Sun** (6 years) From 36.8 years to 42.8 years | | |
|---|---|---|
| Sub-period | Start | End |
| Sun | 11-15-1915 | 03-04-1916 |
| Moon | 03-04-1916 | 09-03-1916 |
| Mars | 09-03-1916 | 01-08-1917 |
| Rahu | 01-08-1917 | 12-03-1917 |
| Jupiter | 12-03-1917 | 09-21-1918 |
| Saturn | 09-21-1918 | 09-03-1919 |
| Mercury | 09-03-1919 | 07-10-1920 |
| Ketu | 07-10-1920 | 11-15-1920 |
| Venus | 11-15-1920 | 11-15-1921 |

| **Ketu** (7 years) From 9.8 years to 16.8 years | | |
|---|---|---|
| Sub-period | Start | End |
| Ketu | 11-14-1888 | 12-04-1889 |
| Venus | 04-12-1889 | 12-06-1890 |
| Sun | 06-12-1890 | 18-10-1890 |
| Moon | 10-18-1890 | 19-05-1891 |
| Mars | 05-19-1891 | 15-10-1891 |
| Rahu | 10-15-1891 | 02-11-1892 |
| Jupiter | 11-02-1892 | 09-10-1893 |
| Saturn | 10-09-1893 | 17-11-1894 |
| Mercury | 11-17-1894 | 15-11-1895 |

| **Moon** (10 years) From 42.8 years to 52.8 years | | |
|---|---|---|
| Sub-period | Start | End |
| Moon | 11-15-1921 | 09-15-1922 |
| Mars | 09-15-1922 | 04-16-1923 |
| Rahu | 04-16-1923 | 10-15-1924 |
| Jupiter | 10-15-1924 | 02-14-1926 |
| Saturn | 02-14-1926 | 09-16-1927 |
| Mercury | 09-16-1927 | 02-14-1929 |
| Ketu | 02-14-1929 | 09-15-1929 |
| Venus | 09-15-1929 | 05-17-1931 |
| Sun | 05-17-1931 | 11-15-1931 |

| **Venus** (20 years) From 16.8 years to 36.8 years | | |
|---|---|---|
| Sub-period | Start | End |
| Venus | 11-15-1895 | 16-03-1899 |
| Sun | 03-16-1899 | 16-03-1900 |
| Moon | 03-16-1900 | 15-11-1901 |
| Mars | 11-15-1901 | 15-01-1903 |
| Rahu | 01-15-1903 | 15-01-1906 |
| Jupiter | 01-15-1906 | 15-09-1908 |
| Saturn | 09-15-1908 | 16-11-1911 |
| Mercury | 11-16-1911 | 15-09-1914 |
| Ketu | 09-15-1914 | 15-11-1915 |

| **Mars** (17 years) From 52.8 years to 59.8 years | | |
|---|---|---|
| Sub-period | Start | End |
| Mars | 11-15-1931 | 04-12-1932 |
| Rahu | 04-12-1932 | 05-01-1933 |
| Jupiter | 05-01-1933 | 04-07-1934 |
| Saturn | 04-07-1934 | 05-17-1935 |
| Mercury | 05-17-1935 | 05-13-1936 |
| Ketu | 05-13-1936 | 10-09-1936 |
| Venus | 10-09-1936 | 12-09-1937 |
| Sun | 12-09-1937 | 04-16-1938 |
| Moon | 04-16-1938 | 11-15-1938 |

| Rahu (18 years) From 59.8 years to 77.8 years | | |
|---|---|---|
| Sub-period | Start | End |
| Rahu | 11-15-1938 | 07-28-1941 |
| Jupiter | 07-28-1941 | 12-22-1943 |
| Saturn | 12-22-1943 | 10-28-1946 |
| Mercury | 10-28-1946 | 05-16-1949 |
| Ketu | 05-16-1949 | 06-04-1950 |
| Venus | 06-04-1950 | 06-03-1953 |
| Sun | 06-03-1953 | 04-28-1954 |
| Moon | 04-28-1954 | 10-28-1955 |
| Mars | 10-28-1955 | 11-14-1956 |

| Jupiter (16 years) From 77.8 years to 93.8 years | | |
|---|---|---|
| Sub-period | Start | End |
| Jupiter | 11-14-1956 | 01-03-1959 |
| Saturn | 01-03-1959 | 07-16-1961 |
| Mercury | 07-16-1961 | 10-22-1963 |
| Ketu | 10-22-1963 | 09-27-1964 |
| Venus | 09-27-1964 | 05-29-1967 |
| Sun | 05-29-1967 | 03-16-1968 |
| Moon | 03-16-1968 | 07-16-1969 |
| Mars | 07-16-1969 | 06-22-1970 |
| Rahu | 06-22-1970 | 11-14-1972 |

| Saturn (19 years) From 93.8 years to 112.8 years | | |
|---|---|---|
| Sub-period | Start | End |
| Saturn | 11-14-1972 | 11-18-1975 |
| Mercury | 11-18-1975 | 07-28-1978 |
| Ketu | 07-28-1978 | 09-06-1979 |
| Venus | 09-06-1979 | 11-06-1982 |
| Sun | 11-06-1982 | 10-19-1983 |
| Moon | 10-19-1983 | 05-19-1985 |
| Mars | 05-19-1985 | 06-28-1986 |
| Rahu | 06-28-1986 | 05-04-1989 |
| Jupiter | 05-04-1989 | 11-15-1991 |

of us to make it around the clock! In one complete cycle, each of the nine planets reigns for a specified and predetermined duration. The starting point for these periods of influence is determined by the position of the Moon in the natal chart, and the constellation in which it is present at the time of birth becomes our lunar birth star. In India it would be considered our birth sign.

The length of the first planetary period is adjusted according to the degree occupied by the Moon in our birth constellation. A planet—along with all the yogas in which it participates—is activated when its period of influence comes into effect, and it readily defines the framework and atmosphere of that slice of one's life.

The planetary cycles are very sensitive to the exact time of one's birth, so that if one's time of birth is inaccurate by even a few minutes, it will affect the layout of the calendar periods. If the events indicated by the planetary cycles do not match the native's experience, there are several methods to check and correct the time of birth, a process that will have to be presented in a later publication though.

The planetary period in which a person is born is of particular importance because it marks one's early life experiences and has a sustained influence on his direction and motivations.

To introduce you to the planets' periods of influence, let's take a look at the stages of Einstein's life as per the previous tables.

## Major Periods and Sub-periods

The order of the planets and the length of their periods of influence are as follows:

| Lord of the Period | Length of the Period |
|---|---|
| Ketu | 7 years |
| Venus | 20 years |
| Sun | 6 years |
| Moon | 10 years |
| Mars | 7 years |
| Rahu | 18 years |
| Jupiter | 16 years |
| Saturn | 19 years |
| Mercury | 17 years |

From the outset it is evident that the planets govern slices of life that vary in length. Moreover, as shown in the table on the following two pages, each of these larger periods is further divided into sub-periods. These can in turn be subdivided into even smaller periods, and so on, in order to better pinpoint the influences active at a particular time of someone's life. Most astrologers, however, consider a maximum of five levels of periods. We will confine ourselves here to three.

For each subsequent level of sub-periods, the planets will exert their influence in the same order as in the table on pages 236-237.

As we have seen, the static analysis of a chart allows us to determine the nature, quality, and extent of the influence of different planets. What we have to do now is look at events that could occur under their auspices in the light of our data.

The following principles guide our interpretation of the planetary periods:

- The planet that governs a given period produces results consistent with its characteristics in the chart.
- Lords of quadrants and trines usually produce favourable results when they govern a period.
- Lords of hidden houses oftentimes produce poor results when they govern a period, unless they are involved in very favourable yogas.

| MAJOR PERIOD | KETU | VENUS | SUN | MOON |
|---|---|---|---|---|
| Sub-periods | KETU | VENUS | SUN | MOON |
| | VENUS | SUN | MOON | MARS |
| | SUN | MOON | MARS | RAHU |
| | MOON | MARS | RAHU | JUPITER |
| | MARS | RAHU | JUPITER | SATURN |
| | RAHU | JUPITER | SATURN | MERCURY |
| | JUPITER | SATURN | MERCURY | KETU |
| | SATURN | MERCURY | KETU | VENUS |
| | MERCURY | KETU | VENUS | SUN |

- Lords of *upachaya* houses (3, 6, 10, and 11) usually produce favourable results towards the end of their period of influence.

- One should also consider the attributes of the ruler of each period in the 9th division.

To better understand the influence of the lord of a major period and that of a sub-period, let's say that the first is like a principal director giving general instructions, and the second, a manager responsible for coordinating resources and giving more detailed instructions. In the same way, the lord of a sub-sub-period would be comparable to a direct supervisor, and so on.

Although the angles of observation from the Ascendant, the Moon, and the Sun are all valid for

| Mars | Rahu | Jupiter | Saturn | Mercury |
|---|---|---|---|---|
| Mars | Rahu | Jupiter | Saturn | Mercury |
| Rahu | Jupiter | Saturn | Mercury | Ketu |
| Jupiter | Saturn | Mercury | Ketu | Venus |
| Saturn | Mercury | Ketu | Venus | Sun |
| Mercury | Ketu | Venus | Sun | Moon |
| Ketu | Venus | Sun | Moon | Mars |
| Venus | Sun | Moon | Mars | Rahu |
| Sun | Moon | Mars | Rahu | Jupiter |
| Moon | Mars | Rahu | Jupiter | Saturn |

assessing the planetary periods, we will here use the following technique:

- The major period will be examined by looking at the position of its lord in relation to the Sun, i.e., the house occupied by the Sun then being treated as the 1st house.

- The sub-period will be studied by looking at the position of its ruler from the Moon's position.

- The sub-sub-period will be studied as a function of the position of its ruler in relation to the Ascendant.

- Let us apply this technique to the chart of our mystery star.

## Exercise 6 – Exploring a Chart

### The Influence of Planetary Periods on Our Mystery Star

Our superstar buckled up the 18 years of her Rahu period in May 2010. The effects of Rahu's bounty, as we have amply observed all along, have left their indelible marks and left her with a host of experiences on which to reminisce. The period extending from April 2009 to May 2010, which was the last sub-period of her Rahu major period, has been a crucial time of transition from one major planetary period to another. During this transition, she has been required to make important decisions about the direction she will take in the future and take the necessary steps to move accordingly—this is also true for all of us when we come to the last sub-period of a major period. So, the choices she made then and the way her mind has evolved set the stage for her next major period, that of Jupiter, which began in May 2010.

We've observed the exchange of constellations between Rahu and Jupiter and have carefully noted how they are both placed in money houses. So, her career will definitively go on albeit, internally, she must now find herself more peaceful and contented as Jupiter is settling into her life. The Rahu period is a typical "no satisfaction" and internally troubled time of life, no matter what success one may attain. Jupiter finally adds that bit of understanding that allows a different perspective on one's worldly attainments and blunders.

By applying our planetary period analysis technique, we'll observe that from the Sun's position, Jupiter is located in the 12th house in Venus' sign of

Libra. This propels relationships to the forefront and should bring in more international business for our star. Being in Libra, Jupiter will activate all the yogas in which Venus participates—and we see that Venus occupies house 3 from the Sun, keeping artistic work a part of her life. Venus also rules the 7th house in Taurus from the solar perspective, which continues to preoccupy her with issues of marriage and business relationships. Jupiter also activates all the yogas in which it plays a part and these, by the way, are all valid from any angle of the chart since there are solar, lunar, and constellation exchanges. The solar yoga, for example, promises gains and eloquence, so we can keep this as a lifetime asset in her "yoga basket." Jupiter very strongly occupies the 10th house of career in the 9th division. Moreover, here also we can find lifetime solar and lunar yogas—as well as a conjunction with money lord Mars. Conclusion: Madame is in no way bound to fade to the realm of bygone stars anytime soon, unless she chooses to or unless some collective cataclysm hits this whole planet.

#### SUB-PERIOD OF JUPITER: MAY 1, 2010 - JUNE 18, 2012

Hail Jupiter who, counting from the Moon in Capricorn, is located in the 10th house of career, being lord of houses 3 and 12—which once again puts arts and international activity in the limelight. As relationships, business, and money schemes remain prominent factors from many angles, our star should successfully output her work and retain her fame during this period.

We've already described Jupiter's glories in the 9th division so, life goes on!

So far we can see that the major period and current sub-period are bound to be very productive, thanks to all the activated yogas. Nonetheless, the influence of the

The influence of planetary periods on our mystery star

| **Moon** (10 years) From 0 year to 3.4 years | | |
|---|---|---|
| Sub-periods | Start | End |
| Moon | | |
| Mars | | |
| Rahu | | |
| Jupiter | | |
| Saturn | | |
| Mercury | 02-12-1981 | 07-31-1982 |
| Ketu | 07-31-1982 | 03-01-1983 |
| Venus | 03-01-1983 | 10-30-1984 |
| Sun | 10-30-1984 | 04-30-1985 |

| **Jupiter** (16 years) From 28.4 years to 44.4 years | | |
|---|---|---|
| Sub-periods | Start | End |
| Jupiter | 04-30-2010 | 06-18-2012 |
| Saturn | 06-18-2012 | 12-30-2014 |
| Mercury | 12-30-2014 | 04-06-2017 |
| Ketu | 04-06-2017 | 03-13-2018 |
| Venus | 03-13-2018 | 11-11-2020 |
| Sun | 11-11-2020 | 08-30-2021 |
| Moon | 08-30-2021 | 12-30-2022 |
| Mars | 12-30-2022 | 12-06-2023 |
| Rahu | 12-06-2023 | 04-30-2026 |

| **Mars** (7 years) From 3.4 years to 10.4 years | | |
|---|---|---|
| Sub-periods | Start | End |
| Mars | 04-30-1985 | 09-27-1985 |
| Rahu | 09-27-1985 | 10-15-1986 |
| Jupiter | 10-15-1986 | 09-21-1987 |
| Saturn | 09-21-1987 | 10-30-1988 |
| Mercury | 10-30-1988 | 10-27-1989 |
| Ketu | 10-27-1989 | 03-25-1990 |
| Venus | 03-25-1990 | 05-25-1991 |
| Sun | 05-25-1991 | 09-30-1991 |
| Moon | 09-30-1991 | 04-30-1992 |

| **Saturn** (19 years) From 44.4 years to 63.4 years | | |
|---|---|---|
| Sub-periods | Start | End |
| Saturn | 04-30-2026 | 05-03-2029 |
| Mercury | 05-03-2029 | 01-11-2032 |
| Ketu | 01-11-2032 | 19-02-2033 |
| Venus | 02-19-2033 | 04-21-2036 |
| Sun | 04-21-2036 | 04-03-2037 |
| Moon | 04-03-2037 | 11-02-2038 |
| Mars | 11-02-2038 | 12-12-2039 |
| Rahu | 12-12-2039 | 10-18-2042 |
| Jupiter | 10-18-2042 | 04-30-2045 |

| **Rahu** (18 years) From 10.4 years to 28.4 years | | |
|---|---|---|
| Sub-periods | Start | End |
| Rahu | 04-30-1992 | 11-01-1995 |
| Jupiter | 01-11-1995 | 01-11-1995 |
| Saturn | 06-06-1997 | 04-12-2000 |
| Mercury | 04-12-2000 | 10-30-2002 |
| Ketu | 10-30-2002 | 11-18-2003 |
| Venus | 11-18-2003 | 11-17-2006 |
| Sun | 11-17-2006 | 10-12-2007 |
| Moon | 10-12-2007 | 04-12-2009 |
| Mars | 04-12-2009 | 04-30-2010 |

| **Mercury** (17 years) From 63.4 years to 80.4 years | | |
|---|---|---|
| Sub-periods | Start | End |
| Mercury | 04-30-2010 | 09-27-2047 |
| Ketu | 09-27-2047 | 09-23-2048 |
| Venus | 09-23-2048 | 07-25-2051 |
| Sun | 07-25-2051 | 05-30-2052 |
| Moon | 05-30-2052 | 10-29-2053 |
| Mars | 10-29-2053 | 10-27-2054 |
| Rahu | 10-27-2054 | 05-15-2057 |
| Jupiter | 05-15-2057 | 08-21-2059 |
| Saturn | 08-21-2059 | 04-30-2062 |

| **Ketu** (7 years) From 80.4 years to 87.4 years | | |
|---|---|---|
| Sub-periods | Start | End |
| Ketu | 04-30-2062 | 09-26-2062 |
| Venus | 09-26-2062 | 11-26-2063 |
| Sun | 11-26-2063 | 04-02-2064 |
| Moon | 04-02-2064 | 11-01-2064 |
| Mars | 11-01-2064 | 03-30-2065 |
| Rahu | 03-30-2065 | 18-04-2066 |
| Jupiter | 04-18-2066 | 04-18-2066 |
| Saturn | 03-25-2067 | 05-03-2068 |
| Mercury | 05-03-2068 | 04-30-2069 |

| **Venus** (20 years) From 87.4 years to 107.4 years | | |
|---|---|---|
| Sub-periods | Start | End |
| Venus | 04-30-2069 | 08-29-2072 |
| Sun | 08-29-2072 | 08-29-2073 |
| Moon | 08-29-2073 | 04-30-2075 |
| Mars | 04-30-2075 | 06-29-2076 |
| Rahu | 06-29-2076 | 06-30-2079 |
| Jupiter | 06-30-2079 | 02-28-2082 |
| Saturn | 02-28-2082 | 04-30-2085 |
| Mercury | 04-30-2085 | 02-28-2088 |
| Ketu | 02-28-2088 | 04-30-2089 |

| **Sun** (6 years) From 107.4 years to 113.4 years | | |
|---|---|---|
| Sub-periods | Start | End |
| Sun | 04-30-2089 | 08-17-2089 |
| Moon | 08-17-2089 | 02-16-2090 |
| Mars | 02-16-2090 | 06-24-2090 |
| Rahu | 06-24-2090 | 05-18-2091 |
| Jupiter | 05-18-2091 | 03-06-2092 |
| Saturn | 03-06-2092 | 02-15-2093 |
| Mercury | 02-15-2093 | 12-23-2093 |
| Ketu | 12-23-2093 | 04-30-2094 |
| Venus | 04-30-2094 | 04-30-2095 |

lunar nodes will still be felt and keep bringing the inevitable turmoil and surprises. In fact, it is the very nature of Rahu and Ketu, as malefics, to turn people's lives into a roller coaster ride by sometimes giving generously and sometimes dropping their victim from great height. However, the nodes will tone down, thanks to Jupiter, and our star will find herself gaining some most welcomed maturity to deal with her eventful life.

### SUB-SUB-PERIOD OF VENUS: MAY 19, 2011 - SEPTEMBER 26, 2011

Lord of houses 2 and 9 from the Ascendant, Venus occupies the 5th house—love, children, investments, creativity, desire—in the ambitious sign of Saturn, himself situated in the Ascendant. Capricorn, in fact, is the very sign of career and work, and all these aspects are therefore active elements during this period of our star's life. Capricorn and Virgo both being earth signs, they often point to some level of wealth being generated when activated as in this case. So we can also clearly smell some interesting income and suspect she's got some new production just ready to release for the pleasure of her admiring fans and the bliss of her bankers.

In the 9th division, Venus occupies the 11th house of gains, ambitions, satisfaction of one's desires, ornaments, and luxury, all important issues that could maybe, even, bring her an engagement ring.

#### THE MATURATION OF THE PLANETS

A word about the maturation of the planets, which was mentioned in Chapter 1. The year 2008 is when our mystery celebrity's Mars came to maturity. As we have already observed, Mars, her soul significator, is afflicted by Rahu and Saturn on either side. Mars is also the planet of confrontation, and so this lady has undergone all kinds of conflicts—legal problems, substance abuse, psychiatric care, and hospitalization.

During the maturation of the Moon (between the ages of 23 and 24), she was married twice—note that the Moon is not only conjoined with Venus, the significator of marriage, but also becomes the lord of the 7th house from its position in Capricorn, not to mention it is also in conjunction with the troublesome lunar nodes, which guarantee setbacks.

### Tips for Exploring Your Own Chart

You are now ready to put a timeframe on the influences you found in your chart. As we have noted, a planet can be both lord of a promising house and of another that causes problems. In such a case, when this planet rules one of your planetary periods, these opposing poles will manifest in your life. For example, for an Aries

Ascendant, Jupiter is the dispositor of houses 9 and 12. It may well provide good luck and progress to the house where it is, but it will also bring costs and pitfalls, whether in love or business. It is therefore important to target your active planets and to consider, as we showed above, their influences from the Ascendant, as well as from the Sun and Moon as Ascendants.

## Transits

Transits correspond to the positions occupied by the planets in their current trajectory, or at the particular time that we want to examine more closely.

Thus, after assessing the influence of the lord of the major period and its sub-periods, we should take the transits into consideration.

The precise points where transiting planets are superimposed on those of the natal chart determine how the horoscope will be affected. The transiting planets influence—either by conjunction or aspect—the elements of the chart, being either favourable or not according to their own nature, as rulers of the houses, and as significators of the most prominent aspects of life such as education, health, and career.

A transit must be evaluated according to the house in the natal chart where the transiting planet is temporarily present. We must also consider the nature of the planet and its attributes as lord of the houses it rules. For example, Saturn transiting the 7th house indicates difficulties for all the meanings of that house. By contrast, if Saturn proves to be benefic in the chart overall, it will create a generally favourable climate, though punctuated with difficulties.

The strength of a transit is often more relevant when the planet approaches the same degree as a planet in the natal chart, and culminates when it reaches the exact same degree. In addition to conjunctions, transiting planets produce aspects, just as they do in the natal chart. Transits, combined with the progress of planetary periods, allow us to identify specific events in the native's everyday life.

When Saturn and Jupiter are opposed to each other by transit, they underlie times of progress in the houses where they transit—although Saturn's position does not promise it will be easy. Progress is also indicated when these two are in trine to each other, that is 5 or 9 houses away from each other.

Transits cannot overrule the planetary periods. They rather flow along with them or present obstacles and aggravations in due course of time.

## A Doubly Striking Example: Einstein

Let us take a look at the planetary periods active on May 29, 1919.

### MAJOR PERIOD OF THE SUN

As we saw earlier, the chart of the great physicist is full of yogas. It follows that the major period of the Sun, located in the 10th house, will especially influence his career, even more so given that this is the house where the Sun attains optimum strength. Nestled snugly between exalted Venus and Mercury, the ruler of the Ascendant—whose fall has been cancelled—the Sun activates the energy of all yogas related to house 10 and its lord, the magnificent Jupiter, which is sitting in house 9. The Sun's conjunction with Saturn deepens the native's focus on his goals. It may also be mentioned that Venus and Mercury are both significators of mathematics.

In the Moon chart, the Sun rules house 10 in the 5th—opportunity, creativity, and intelligence. Since the Sun represents prestige and authority among other things, it is not surprising that this period was very productive for Einstein, culminating in the awarding of a Nobel Prize. In the 9th division, the Sun occupies the 5th house facing a full Moon, which also helps to maintain its positive influence throughout this entire period.

### SUB-PERIOD OF SATURN

From the Ascendant, Saturn is involved in several yogas in conjunction with the 10th house, related to career. We also note that Saturn is the dispositor of Mars, which is exalted in Capricorn in the 8th house—secrets and mysteries. This period of Saturn therefore stimulates the influence of Mars, which then becomes a very active success factor.

Planetary periods around the transits of May 29, 1919

| Sun - Saturn | | |
|---|---|---|
| Sub-period | Start | End |
| Saturne | 09-21-1918 | 11-15-1918 |
| Mercure | 11-15-1918 | 01-04-1919 |
| Kétou | 01-04-1919 | 01-24-1919 |
| Vénus | 01-24-1919 | 03-23-1919 |
| Soleil | 03-23-1919 | 04-09-1919 |
| Lune | 04-09-1919 | 05-08-1919 |
| Mars | 05-08-1919 | 05-28-1919 |
| Rahou | 05-28-1919 | 07-19-1919 |
| Jupiter | 07-19-1919 | 09-03-1919 |

From the Moon, Saturn, representing concentration and success through hard work, occupies house 5—intelligence—as lord of house 4 and participates in several yogas. Like the Sun, Saturn is surrounded by benefics conferring positive attributes. It follows that Saturn has taken an active part in the success of Mr. Einstein from that position as well.

### SUB-SUB-PERIOD OF RAHU

Rahu represents obsessions and cravings, and gives Einstein a lot of ambition and motivation. Rahu also represents technical skills, science in general, and the profession of physicist. So it appears that its qualities, conjoined with those of Mars—which represents energy and the pioneering spirit—exalted in the sign of perseverance, Capricorn, in house 8—mysticism and the unknown—have borne fruit. Indeed, Rahu acts like Saturn here and amplifies the qualities of Mars, to the point that the conjunction of these two malefics creates a raw and even explosive energy—one that also contributed to the invention of the atomic bomb! Being in the sign of Saturn, these two planets express themselves with determination and discipline, relentlessly, even compulsively. This combination also stimulates Saturn, creating a strong link between research and career and instilling a profound desire to decipher the laws of the universe, which ultimately left Mr. Einstein deeply moved by the underlying intelligence of the creation.

### APPLYING TRANSITS

We give here the example of the transits that were in effect during the solar eclipse of May 29, 1919 in Berlin, Germany. On that fateful day, the theories of Sir Isaac Newton about our universe were shelved after one of the presumptions of Albert Einstein related to the theory of relativity was tested and produced positive

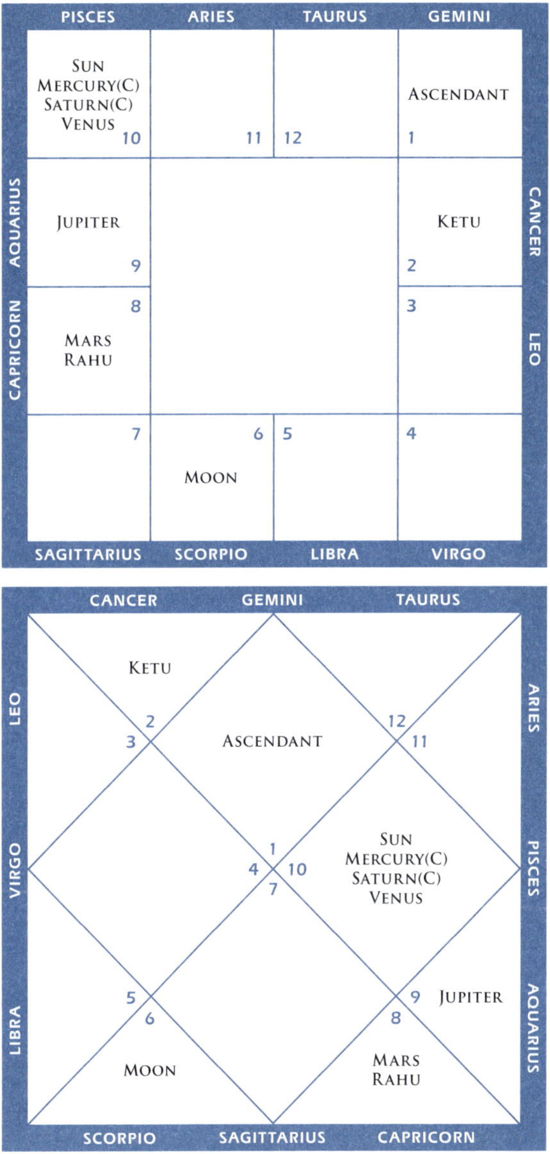


Natal chart — Albert Einstein

Transits during the eclipse of May 29, 1919

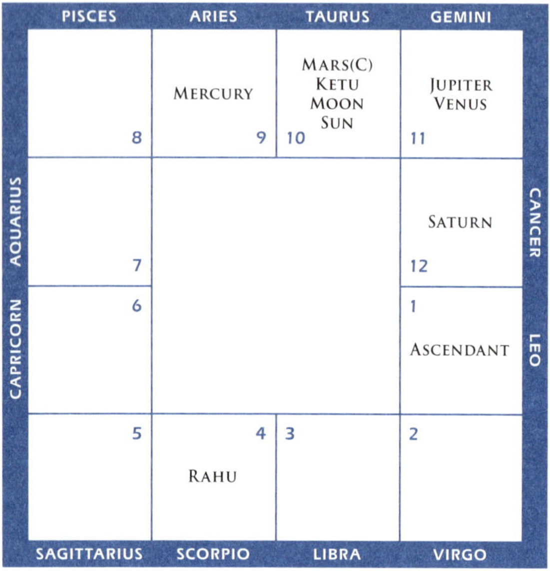


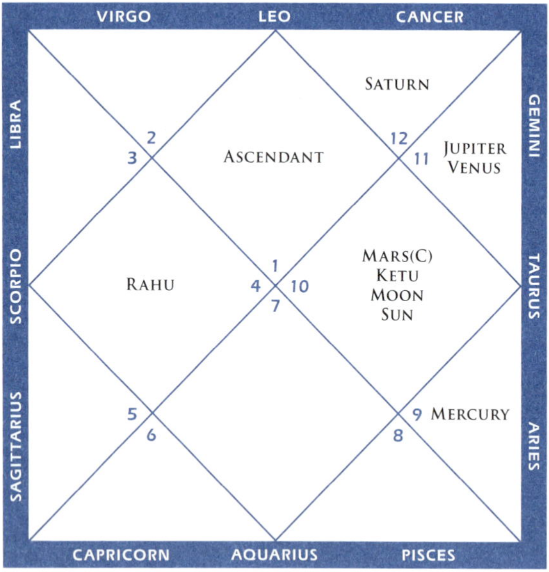

results. Mr. Einstein at once became a hero of international stature.

An eclipse may mark a major shift in our lives and the world, and this particular eclipse proved to be significant for both Albert Einstein and all of us. An eclipse underlines the power of the lunar nodes, representing random events and the karma that must take its course. When an eclipse occurs, the lunar nodes dominate the luminaries—the Sun and Moon—and cover them in darkness, proving they can be smarter than them.

During the eclipse of May 29, 1919, Venus, exalted in the 10th house of Einstein's natal chart, was conjoined, in transit, with Jupiter, the lord of the 10th. This conjunction between two benefics occurred in the sign of Gemini, Einstein's Ascendant, and greatly helped propel him to the world's center stage.

By examining the aspects resulting from the transits, we see that Jupiter and Venus were aspecting the 10th house through the sign they occupied. From the position of the Sun, Jupiter and Venus directly aspected the 10th house, in Sagittarius. And, what is more, Jupiter also aspects houses 5 and 9 of the natal chart, in Libra and Aquarius, respectively. A winning transit!

## Exercise 7 – Exploring a Chart

### The Influence of Transits on Our Mystery Star

Before we dive into our celebrity's transits coupled with the planetary periods, let's just rewind to the last crucial

Natal chart — Mystery star

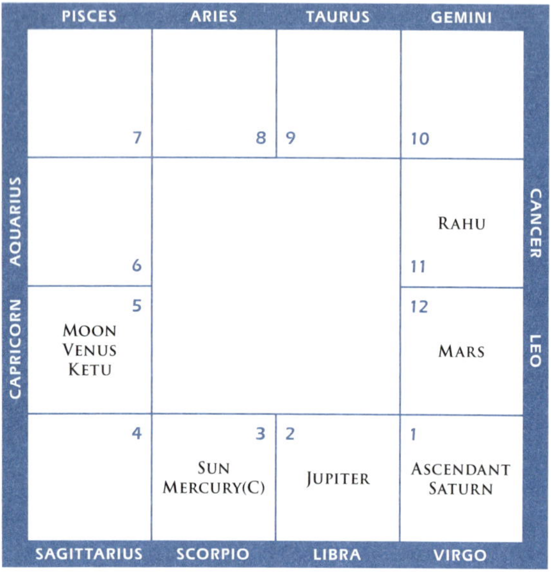


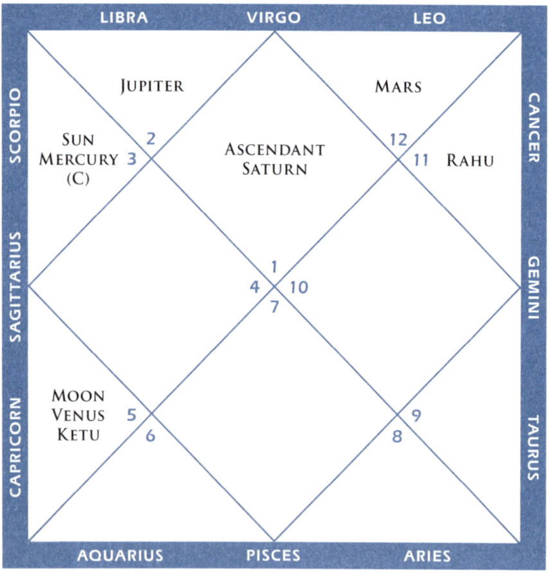

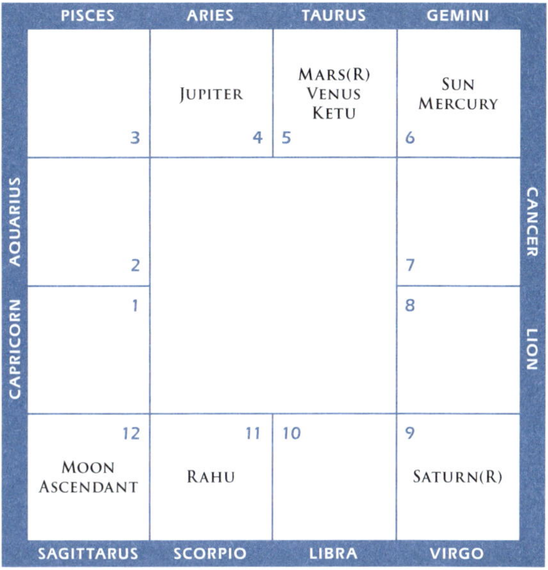


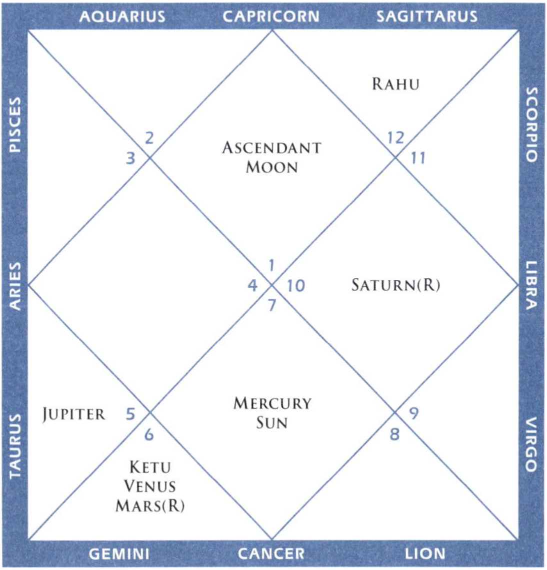


Transits during the total lunar eclipse of June 15, 2011

sub-period of her 18-year Rahu period. This sub-period, from April 2009 to May 2010, was ruled by Mars, her soul significator, situated in her 12th house of foreign affairs—this is the time when she made a splash with her first worldwide tour. We should know that Saturn was then transiting Leo in her 12th house while Jupiter benevolently smiled on the scene from Aquarius, across the chart. To add to this, the nodes were over her houses 5 and 11—entertainments and profits!

#### JUPITER, LORD OF THE MAJOR PERIOD

At the time of the total lunar eclipse of June 15, 2011, Jupiter occupied Aries by transit. It thus activated our star's 8th house—mysteries, unearned income, and subconscious—and aspected her 2nd house of finances and accumulated wealth, speech, etc. This Jupiter transit should have proved to be lucrative to her already profitable natal affairs—the few weeks prior to the eclipse should have been especially good for income and success as transiting Jupiter was facing natal Jupiter to the exact degree.

At this very time, Saturn, lord of Capricorn, was stationed over her Ascendant and aspected her natal Sun to the degree—this must have been a time for hard work and limelight but would also have affected her ego, body, or father with possibilities of losses as the Sun rules the 12th house. Since this is a lunar eclipse, we may opt for something related to perceptions, which points to her ego as a function of the mental body. Whatever may be the case, due to its slow and changing motion, transiting Saturn directly aspected her natal Sun for some 6 weeks so, she should have felt the crunch. And, sorry to say, transiting Jupiter did not keep transiting Saturn in check by a benevolent aspect, neither did it aspect natal Sun. Moreover, transiting

Rahu had just moved into Scorpio and Mars was directly aspecting Scorpio, the Sun, and Mercury, her Ascendant lord, from its position in Taurus. Four malefics afflicting... very crunchy indeed—time for a little health watch.

The Rahu/Ketu axis will be on our star's houses 3 and 9 where artistic work is produced and then brought out to the public with their usual surprises until December 2012.

JUPITER, LORD OF THE SUB-PERIOD

Same as above...

VENUS, LORD OF THE SUB-SUB-PERIOD

Transiting Venus occupied Taurus, its own sign, which is our celebrity's 9th house. But it was, along with natal 9th house, afflicted by Mars and the nodes of the Moon. So most likely, around this time period, along with her success there were also set-backs, conflicts, and certainly critics, which are part of an artist's life. But, the pay is good!

Planetary periods around the transits of June 15, 2011

| Jupiter-Jupiter | | |
|---|---|---|
| Sub-sub-period | Start | End |
| Jupiter | 05-01-2010 | 08-12-2010 |
| Saturn | 08-13-2010 | 12-13-2010 |
| Mercury | 12-14-2010 | 04-03-2011 |
| Ketu | 04-04-2011 | 05-18-2011 |
| Venus | 05-19-2011 | 09-25-2011 |
| Sun | 09-26-2011 | 11-03-2011 |
| Moon | 11-04-2011 | 01-07-2012 |
| Mars | 01-08-2011 | 02-21-2012 |
| Rahu | 02-22-2012 | 06-17-2012 |

By visiting *www.yourvedicastrology.com/book1*, you can find, along with tools to obtain your birth chart, the current state of the transits and apply them to your own astrological chart. The positions of Saturn, Jupiter, Rahu, and Ketu are particularly important to note, since their influence lasts longer: two and a half years for Saturn, 18 months for Rahu and Ketu, and generally one year for Jupiter.

If you find that Saturn is conjoined with the natal Moon by transit, or is even in one of the immediately adjoining houses, then you are in a period called *Sade Sati*. This is the period of Saturn's influence, which lasts about seven and a half years and can return as many as three times over the course of a lifetime. During these periods, you must stay alert and exercise more prudence and discretion than usual, because these years are generally full of difficult obstacles to overcome, pervasive torment, and even depression on the negative side; but they can also act as catalysts to uplift one materially and spiritually.

If Jupiter is conjoined with your natal Moon by transit, life will be kinder.

A situation where Mars and Rahu/Ketu, or Saturn are transiting a major house could provoke accidents, setbacks, conflicts, confusion, or unexpected events.

By contrast, benefics aspecting propitious points of the chart by transit most often produce excellent results, unless they themselves are quite afflicted as in our example above.

# CHAPTER 7

# ANTIDOTES

Since nothing is ever perfect in this world, and each chart shows different strengths and weaknesses, Vedic science offers us remedies to overcome, or at least alleviate negative planetary influences, as well as to stimulate positive influences to which we are exposed. These antidotes are one of the major differences between Vedic and Western astrology.

As Vedic astrology helps us to anticipate upcoming positive or negative events, we can use these antidotes to increase our resistance or tolerance to negative influences, while maximizing promising opportunities and our ability to take advantage of them. Since the planets are the active principles in the firmament, their movements and location in a chart also clearly indicate in what areas future events will occur.

It goes without saying that the Vedic antidotes are not a panacea for all our problems. Thus, in case of illness, for example, it is best to consult a physician. Similarly, if our problems are rooted in bad habits, we must first and foremost take appropriate steps to correct them, while using the prescribed astrological remedy to help offset the planetary weakness that has contributed to our taking on such patterns of behaviour.

Since a single planet can simultaneously affect different areas of our lives, we must also ensure that the proposed antidote for a given problem does not create other imbalances in the ecosystem of a chart.

Finally, let us remember that the karma associated with the movable signs is easier to correct, because these signs naturally favour change. Karma connected to the dual signs is somewhat flexible, but not that easy to correct. And karma related to the fixed signs offers even more resistance and may sometimes require significant remedial efforts.

## Selecting Auspicious Days

A simple corrective measure may be to select specific days of the week to perform certain activities, because every day is associated with a planet. Moreover, with regard to the antidotes that follow, it is recommended to start using them on the day of the planet whose influence we want to pacify. These are the days corresponding to the planets:

- **Sunday**: Sun – individuality and vitality;
- **Monday**: Moon – perceptions and emotions;
- **Tuesday**: Mars – action and confrontation;
- **Wednesday**: Mercury – communication, discernment, and intellectual endeavours;
- **Thursday**: Jupiter – morality, wisdom, and prosperity;
- **Friday**: Venus – arts, love, and pleasures;
- **Saturday**: Saturn – discipline, concentration, and life lessons.

For example, Sunday is the traditional day to visit a temple, church, or place of worship in many traditions, which is in line with the significations of the Sun.

Similarly, the day of Mars is prescribed when it comes to exercising initiative.

And as for meeting with your new lover or to go out and relax, the day of Venus opens the gate for pleasures.

## Natural Gemstones

Natural gemstones, worn as jewellery, are also classic antidotes. When combined with sincere efforts to improve one's way of life and to raise one's consciousness, they can be used to take maximum advantage of the energy of different planets. Since every astrological chart is unique, you should target those aspects of your life on which you want to work. Listed below are the gemstones associated with each planet as well as their substitutes:

- **Sun**: ruby • spinel, garnet, sunstone, red zircon, red tourmaline;
- **Moon**: pearl • cultured pearl, moonstone;
- **Mars**: red coral • carnelian, red jasper;
- **Mercury**: emerald • aquamarine, peridot, jade, green zircon, green tourmaline;
- **Jupiter**: yellow sapphire • yellow topaz, citrine, yellow zircon, yellow tourmaline;

- **Venus**: diamond • white sapphire, clear zircon, crystal, white coral;
- **Saturn**: blue sapphire • lapis lazuli, amethyst, turquoise, blue zircon, blue tourmaline;
- **Rahu**: red garnet • honey-coloured garnet, onyx, or zircon;
- **Ketu**: cat's-eye • turquoise, quartz-type cat's-eyes.

Wearing one or more stones related to the Ascendant is particularly appropriate because these gems help reinforce its positive expression.

## Colours

Therapy based on colours related to the planets is a simple process, because the influence of each planet can be increased by exposure to the colour that corresponds to it or, if need be, counteracted by opposing ones. Especially effective for alleviating emotional and psychological imbalances, appropriate colours can be added to one's environment or used in visualization exercises. This form of therapy is also used in the treatment of physical illnesses, especially when the blood, nerves, and reproductive system are affected, in which case one should wear the appropriate colours to alleviate these conditions. For example, an inflammatory disease can be reduced by the use of soothing colours such as white and shades of blue or pale green. Here are the basic colours for each planet:

- **Sun**: transparent red;
- **Moon**: opaque white;
- **Mars**: opaque red;
- **Mercury**: green;
- **Jupiter**: yellow;
- **Venus**: transparent white;
- **Saturn**: blue;
- **Rahu**: ultraviolet, smoky gray, or black;
- **Ketu**: infrared, bright red, or orange.

As you can see, the always fashionable black is only recommended for Rahu, who is said to act as Saturn. In fact, this "colour" accentuates Saturn's negativity, a good thing to know if you need more problems in your life… We should also remember that overall, the planets more easily transmit their positive influence when colours are used in their pure tones, and it is always best to opt for clothing made from natural fibres. More diluted colours will tend to reflect the negative side of the planets.

Note, finally, that in the case of more demanding or restrictive karmas, other antidotes exist in the form of meditation, mantras, chants, prayers, charitable deeds, or the performance of ritual ceremonies.

## ANTIDOTES FOR OUR MYSTERY STAR

Now let us propose some remedies for the ills that we have identified in the chart of our mystery star. Have you guessed who she is yet? It was Britney Spears, of course!

As the Ascendant is in Virgo and as she can afford it, Britney would benefit from wearing a high quality emerald of approximately five carats.

Moreover, as we have now found more than once, her emotions would benefit greatly from a shot of colour! Visualization exercises of soothing images of white, green, and yellow, like a landscape with a bright sun, forests, or fields for the various shades of green, with a huge white fountain dispensing pure water and where birds like to drink.

The eminent professor Robert Koch, who kindly wrote the preface to this book, spotted in Britney Spears' chart the yoga of an ascetic which is again repeated in the 9th division. He observed that our star must have practiced great austerities in past lives for her to have the beauty, prestige, talent, and wealth that she has in this one. Nevertheless, the fact remains that her chart also reveals many afflictions, as we have clearly shown. Those that affect Mars, her soul significator, occur in Leo, a fixed sign, and those that relate to the Sun and Mercury occur in Scorpio, another fixed sign. These positions make a reversal of any resulting karma very difficult. As Britney is deeply affected on a personal level, she would be well advised to undertake a serious spiritual quest to improve these influences. This would, however, require her to change many of her life habits.

Does not Britney Spears' persona as the most insanely sexy virgin in the world, marketed with great virtuosity by her marketing experts, remind us of the kind of religious leader who does not practice what he assures us is the truth? Still, her foreign fans, deceived or not, continue to be a good source of income!

Furthermore, using a technique that we could not include in this introductory book about the essential basics of Vedic astrology, her "derived" Ascendant is in Capricorn, as is the Moon. And this gives a certain indication of how she will be perceived in society, which lends more weight to the position of Saturn in the Moon chart, where it occupies the 9th house of religion or worship, if you will.

Completely deprived of a normal life since childhood (her major period of Rahu began when she was 10 years old), Britney has had to live in a sort of televised tornado with only a one-year break between her tender age and her life as a singer, when at 17, she became the angelic sexy diva who conquered the world. We may rightly wonder about her parents—did they push her toward success, or were they only helping her to fulfill her own personal desire in her early career? Given the afflictions of the Moon and the Sun, we know that her parents were not easy people to live with and that they undoubtedly left her with emotional wounds, and all this might entail. However, it is also clear that her destiny was mapped out in advance, including her marital difficulties and all the rest.

As we mentioned earlier, given the maturity of Mars in 2008, that year promised to feature all sorts of troubles, even more so since Mars occupies its "death" degree, from where it could not provide stable support. Mars' dispositor, the Sun, also landed in its "death" degree, which made this whole period like walking on (rotten) eggs.

Like everyone else on this planet, Britney is not immune to the current social and economic factors that influence everything that lives... and everything that dies! But like all of us, she keeps that partial free will in her attitude towards the joys and sorrows that life brings and can only try her best to evolve spiritually in the context of her life here on earth.

The transit of Saturn in Virgo, her Ascendant, from September 2009 to November 2011, is an ideal time for discipline, sobriety, and for her to take responsibility for herself. If she does not adopt the program that Saturn sets for her at this time, then she risks physical ailments, adversity, or melancholy.

Whatever happens, one thing is for sure: wearing pink will not be enough to solve her problems!

# CONCLUSION

After studying various factors that influence our destiny and may even appear to determine it, it is natural to ask how much free will we have in all this.

As free will is the ability to choose and decide for oneself, it follows that we will be much better equipped to do so, first and foremost, if we know our options.

For example, when buying a car, different approaches can be adopted: one can look at the price, or the car's appearance, or compare different models. Most would probably agree that this last approach is one that allows for the most enlightened choice.

All the Vedic sciences are designed to give us knowledge of the facts and present the options available to us so that we can improve our lives. Vedic astrology is particularly valuable in this regard because it delivers a large amount of data about yourself all at once so that you can readily know both your potential and your limitations. You can thus better orient your life and control your destiny, while maximizing your ability to choose.

To enjoy a maximum of free will in our lives, we must first know who we really are, why we exist, what our karmic tendencies are, and what preventive measures we can take against undesired influences, or even the remedies that can definitively put an end to our karma. This is surely the greatest adventure a human being can live.

Are you ready to take it up?

# ABOUT THE AUTHOR

Andrée Leclerc was born in a typical small Quebec village, Saint-Louis de Lotbinière, in 1962, and from a very early age began to demonstrate a fascination for various aspects of spirituality and Vedic culture.

While still a young girl, she would make a daily visit to the village monastery, and by the age of 11 had already read the *Bhagavad-Gita*. This led her to want to become a vegetarian and live according to the powerful teachings of this book of wisdom, a desire she was finally able to realize when she joined an ashram at the age of 20.

Ever since then, she has been deepening her knowledge of the various branches of Vedic learning, even while remaining in North America, raising and home-schooling two children through most of their primary grades.

A student and practitioner of Vedic philosophy for 25 years, she was awarded the prestigious Siddhanta Shiromani title by Dr. Satya Narayana Dasa, director of the Jiva Institute (India), for her scholarly achievements in Vedic astrology, Ayurveda, devotional Vedanta, mantras, and rituals.

Over the course of time, Vedic astrology has increasingly become her dominant interest. As she learned how to apply this ancient science in daily life, she came to particularly appreciate the way in which it helped her better know and understand the people around her, giving her unique insights both into their lives and each person's prospects for fulfillment.

She began to study nearly everything that has been published on the subject in English. She also attended Vedic astrology conferences where she met some of the best teachers in the field, from whom she has been able to take private instruction in North America and India.

With the help of her valuable associates, she has created two websites, AstrologieVedique.com in French and YourVedicAstrology.com in English in order to provide relevant information to astro lovers.

She is also the founder of a company offering jewellery made of natural gemstones for which she has created nearly 2000 designs. These stones have been used by the Vedic astrologers of India since time immemorial to promote physical, mental, and spiritual well-being.

Her proven mastery of the most important branches of Vedic culture, coupled with her experience as a mother and an entrepreneur, put Andrée Leclerc in a unique position to pass on her knowledge in a practical and relevant manner for the benefit of the largest number of people.

## IN THE SAME SERIES

***Tales of Ancient India***
*Practical Wisdom* — Guy Tétreault
ISBN 978-2-922417-66-1

***Discovering the Absolute***
*Getting to the True Meaning of Life* — Pierre Corbeil
ISBN 978-2-922417-64-7

***The Teachings of Krishna***
*An Ageless Dialog* — Pierre Corbeil
ISBN 978-2-922417-59-3

# TABLES AND GRAPHS

MIX
Paper from
responsible sources
FSC® C011825

This work was printed
on September 9, 2011
by Transcontinental Métrolitho,
Sherbrooke, Canada, for IQ Press